LIVING WITH LEARNING DISABILITIES AND DISORDERS

By Peter Kogler

Portions of this book originally appeared in *Learning Disabilities* by Meryl Loonin.

Published in 2020 by
Lucent Press, an Imprint of Greenhaven Publishing, LLC
353 3rd Avenue
Suite 255
New York, NY 10010

Designer: Deanna Paternostro
Editor: Jennifer Lombardo

Cataloging-in-Publication Data

Names: Kogler, Peter.
Title: Living with learning disabilities and disorders / Peter Kogler.
Description: New York : Lucent Press, 2020. | Series: Diseases and disorders
  | Includes glossary and index.
Identifiers: ISBN 9781534567474 (pbk.) | ISBN 9781534566897 (library bound) | ISBN
  9781534567481 (ebook)
Subjects: LCSH: Learning disabilities–Juvenile literature. | Learning disabled
  teenagers–Education–Juvenile literature.
Classification: LCC LC4704.74 K64 2020 | DDC 371.9–dc23

Printed in the United States of America

CPSIA compliance information: Batch #BS19KL: For further information contact Greenhaven Publishing LLC, New York, New York, at 1-844-317-7404.

Please visit our website, www.greenhavenpublishing.com. For a free color catalog of all our high-quality books, call toll free 1-844-317-7404 or fax 1-844-317-7405.

CONTENTS

FOREWORD

Illness is an unfortunate part of life, and it is one that is often misunderstood. Thanks to advances in science and technology, people have been aware for many years that diseases such as the flu, pneumonia, and chickenpox are caused by viruses and bacteria. These diseases all cause physical symptoms that people can see and understand, and many people have dealt with these diseases themselves. However, sometimes diseases that were previously unknown in most of the world turn into epidemics and spread across the globe. Without an awareness of the method by which these diseases are spread—through the air, through human waste or fluids, through sexual contact, or by some other method—people cannot take the proper precautions to prevent further contamination. Panic often accompanies epidemics as a result of this lack of knowledge.

Knowledge is power in the case of mental disorders, as well. Mental disorders are just as common as physical disorders, but due to a lack of awareness among the general public, they are often stigmatized. Scientists have studied them for years and have found that they are generally caused by chemical imbalances in the brain, but they have not yet determined with certainty what causes those imbalances or how to fix them. Because even mild mental illness is stigmatized in Western society, many people prefer not to talk about it.

Chronic pain disorders are also not well understood—even by researchers—and do not yet have foolproof treatments. People who have a mental disorder or a disease or disorder that causes them to feel chronic pain can be the target of uninformed opinions. People who do not have these disorders sometimes struggle to understand how difficult it can be to deal with the symptoms. These disorders are often termed "invisible illnesses" because no one can see the symptoms; this leads many people to doubt that they exist or are serious problems. Additionally, people who have an undiagnosed disorder may understand that they are experiencing the world in a different way than their peers, but they have no one to turn to for answers.

Misinformation about all kinds of ailments is often spread through personal anecdotes, social media, and even news sources. This series aims to present accurate information about both physical and mental conditions so young adults will have a better understanding of them. Each volume discusses the symptoms of a particular disease or disorder, ways it is currently being treated, and the research that is being done to understand it further. Advice for people who may be suffering from a disorder is included, as well as information for their loved ones about how best to support them.

With fully cited quotes, a list of recommended books and websites for further research, and informational charts, this series provides young adults with a factual introduction to common illnesses. By learning more about these ailments, they will be better able to prevent the spread of contagious diseases, show compassion to people who are dealing with invisible illnesses, and take charge of their own health.

HIDDEN DISABILITIES

Daniel Radcliffe had dreamed about being an actor since he was five years old, but he never saw himself as talented or smart. He found school difficult; handwriting was nearly impossible, and even tying his shoes was not easy for him. These two seemingly simple tasks were out of his reach, and his confidence suffered because of it. His mother initially rejected his dream of becoming an actor. Eventually, however, she allowed her son to audition for a role on a television show in the hope that it would give her son the motivation he so desperately needed.

Radcliffe's experiences are not uncommon. He suffers from a learning disability called dyspraxia, and it still affects him to this day. According to the Eunice Kennedy Shriver National Institute of Child Health and Human Development, part of the National Institutes of Health (NIH), "Learning disabilities affect how a person learns to read, write, speak, and do math. They are caused by differences in the brain, most often in how it functions but also sometimes in its structure. These differences affect the way the brain processes information."[1] In Radcliffe's case, his learning disability affected his motor skills—skills that are directly linked to handwriting and tying shoes.

People who suffer from learning disabilities might sometimes feel stupid or untalented. However, according to the NIH, "A learning disability is not an indication of a person's intelligence. Learning

Despite being diagnosed with dyspraxia, Daniel Radcliffe has become a popular and successful actor.

disabilities are different from learning problems due to intellectual and developmental disabilities, or emotional, vision, hearing, or motor skills problems."[2] Furthermore, the Learning Disabilities Association of America (LDA) reported, "Generally speaking, people with learning disabilities are of average or above average intelligence. … This is why learning disabilities are referred to as 'hidden disabilities': the person looks perfectly 'normal' and seems to be a very bright and intelligent person, yet may be unable to demonstrate the skill level expected from someone of a similar age."[3]

The term "learning disabilities" covers a variety of different disorders, but it is important to note that autism and attention-deficit/hyperactivity disorder (ADHD) are not learning disabilities, despite the fact that they sometimes have similar symptoms. Learning disabilities are incurable and invisible, and they last throughout a person's life. With the right educational and emotional supports, however, those with learning disabilities can go on to live full, happy, and successful lives. By receiving academic and emotional support as children, individuals with a learning disability learn the skills they need to reach their full potential. Unfortunately, because these are hidden disabilities, they can sometimes go unnoticed—and therefore untreated—for a period of time.

Learning Disabilities and Public Perception

According to the NIH, "Because there are many different types of learning disabilities, and some people may have more than one, it is hard to estimate how many people might have learning disabilities."[4] Recent estimates suggest that 1 out of every 5 American children has a learning disability. However, despite the fact that they are so widespread, they are incredibly misunderstood. In 2010, the Emily Hall Tremaine Foundation completed a study on public attitudes about children with learning disabilities. Their findings about the public's perception were far from ideal. According to their research, "Seven out of 10 parents, educators and members of the general public incorrectly link learning disabilities with intellectual disability ('mental retardation') and autism. Half or more of school administrators do so as well." Furthermore, "Almost four in 10 mistakenly associate learning disabilities with sensory impairments like blindness and deafness."[5] Because so many learning disabilities go undetected and misdiagnosed, there are many students who suffer needlessly.

One-third of these students will have to repeat a grade at some point, and an estimated one in two students with learning disabilities will face expulsion or suspension from school. Only about 68 percent of students with a learning disability will graduate with a high school diploma; the rest either drop out or receive a certificate of completion, which is awarded when someone attends high school for all four years but does not meet all the requirements to graduate. Not all colleges accept students with a certificate of completion the way they accept those with a diploma. As adults, about 8 percent are unemployed, and 46 percent report neither working nor seeking work. Of those who are employed, only 5 percent report receiving resources and accommodations in the workplace that make their jobs easier to perform. However, people with learning disabilities are not doomed to failure. Countless people with learning disabilities become doctors, lawyers, writers, athletes, scientists, political leaders, and more. Along with Daniel Radcliffe, Whoopi Goldberg, Steven Spielberg, Tim Tebow, and Justin Timberlake are just a few celebrities who have struggled—and continue to struggle—with learning disabilities in their adult lives. Having a strong support system early on is key for those with a learning disability.

The Importance of Strong Support Systems

A child who is diagnosed with a learning disability today has a much greater chance of succeeding in school and in life than at any time in the past. With advances in technology, researchers have begun to understand more about how learning takes place in the brain. Educators, parents, and school districts as a whole have developed effective strategies and interventions to identify and support these students. Federal laws protect them from discrimination and ensure that they are included in regular education classrooms. Technologies such as assistive listening systems and text-to-speech software also make it easier to help students with a learning disability achieve their goals. However, despite such gains, many of these students report feeling frustrated, insecure, and angry in school.

A learning disability is not a disease. While diseases can be cured or treated with medicine, learning disabilities cannot. A learning disability is often classified as a disorder, but researchers stress the importance of not viewing a person in terms of their disorder. People with learning disabilities are simply individuals who

Direction, guidance, and support are just a few key things that can make a difference in the lives of individuals with learning disabilities.

learn differently than others. They are not, in any way, less smart than their peers or incapable of learning. In fact, some schools integrate students with and without learning disabilities to encourage better learning environments. With a strong support system made up of families, friends, teachers, and the larger community, these individuals can develop a better understanding of how they learn best and what they need to make daily life easier for them.

CHAPTER ONE

A COMPLICATED DEFINITION

The term "learning disability" refers to a range of conditions in the brain that make it difficult for people to learn. It is hard to pin down an exact definition because a learning disability can affect many skills, including reading, writing, speaking, listening, reasoning, solving math problems, coordinating muscle movements, and interacting socially. People who have a learning disability process information differently than other people, because their brains have been found to be "wired," or structured, differently than others. This difference in brain processing interferes with the learning process. For a student with a learning disability, simply trying to read a textbook, write a report, or solve a math problem can be like driving down a road that is packed with slow-moving traffic. Performing these academic tasks causes information to slow down or get "stuck" while traveling through certain parts of the brain.

There is another reason why the term "learning disability" is hard to define. Even if two people have the same learning disability, they will generally not experience the same exact challenges, so the definition of their learning disability is not always a perfect fit. Each individual has a unique pattern of strengths and weaknesses, so their challenges will vary. Some people struggle with a single area of learning, while others have difficulty with several different areas. The ways they learn how to read and spell, add and subtract, tell time, or follow directions will also vary from person to person. The impacts of their learning disabilities and the effects on their everyday life vary from mild to severe.

While everyone with a learning disability is unique, there are certain characteristics that they do have in common. One is that they are intelligent and have the capacity to learn. To be identified as learning disabled, a person must perform in the near average, average, or above average range on a standardized test of intelligence. However, because of their disabilities, there is a gap between what they are capable of achieving and what they actually achieve in school and at work. This is often frustrating to the individual as well as the people around them. Another common characteristic is that these learning disabilities are lifelong. People may develop strategies to compensate for areas of weakness, but their disabilities will not be cured or disappear, even as they grow older.

It is important to note that people from all backgrounds can have learning disabilities. According to Dr. Sheldon Horowitz of the National Center for Learning Disabilities, "Race, culture, economic status—LD [learning disability] doesn't discriminate. It's real and affects people of all ages."[6]

The Three Steps of Learning

When a person has a learning disability, there is a breakdown somewhere in the learning process as information travels through the brain. Researchers sometimes describe the brain as if it were a sophisticated computer system. In such a model, there are three steps that must happen for learning to occur: input, storage, and output. Dr. Larry Silver, a psychiatrist who studies and writes about children with learning disabilities, described the steps of the learning process:

The first step is input, getting information into the brain, primarily from the eyes and the ears. Once this information has arrived, the brain needs to make sense out of it, a process called integration. Next, the information must be stored and later retrieved, the memory process. Finally, the brain must send some kind of message back to the nerves and muscles—its output.[7]

Learning, however, occurs in ways that vary from person to person. The brain is far more complex than a computer because it is actively finding new meaning in the information that arrives from a person's senses. In the first step of the learning process, input, the brain takes in sensory information from the eyes, ears, and other senses. A person with a disability that disrupts the input step may see and hear perfectly well. The problem lies in the brain's ability to perceive things, or how the brain receives the information that arrives through its visual or auditory pathways.

A perception problem can interfere with learning to read, write, solve math equations, or coordinate movements. If the breakdown is in visual perception, a person might confuse the position and shape of letters and numbers or struggle to distinguish an object in the foreground of a picture from those in the background. They might also misjudge distances and constantly bump into things. If the problem interferes with auditory input, they might have trouble telling the difference between similar sounds or hearing what a teacher or classmate is saying over the background noise from the other students in the class.

When the brain stores information, it tries to make sense of new information and compares it with information that it has already received. This process is called integration. The first step to integrating information is called sequencing. A person who struggles with sequencing might perceive letters and words

Recognizing Learning Disabilities

Children with learning disabilities can exhibit a variety of signs and symptoms, both at school and at home. While some teachers and parents may think the child has problems with motivation and behavior, others may notice that a learning disability might be to blame. In preschool, learning disabilities may take the form of poor motor skills, such as difficulty using scissors or coloring with crayons. There can be speech delays, which make understanding and speaking language incredibly frustrating. When multi-step instructions are not being followed and when a child cannot speak about what is on their mind, it can lead to confusion and aggravation for both the child and the adult.

In elementary school, these symptoms increase and compound the issues that occurred in preschool. Because speaking and understanding language was difficult before, the process of learning how to read can be just as frustrating. An increase in the student's workload—such as homework, essays, and student presentations—can begin to affect their grades. Students with a learning disability who have difficulty reading, writing, and speaking typically struggle to complete such assignments and projects. Ideally, teachers and parents who notice these problems will refer the student for an evaluation.

Evaluations help diagnose specific learning disabilities. Once a learning disability is diagnosed, an educational plan that is specifically designed for that student can be put in place. These special education plans will set goals for the student, teacher, and parents to reach together. However, if these learning disabilities are left untreated, the student will be unable to learn the skills they need to navigate successfully through school, college, and even work. Every child deserves an equal chance to succeed both academically and in their everyday life.

in the wrong order—for example, they may perceive the letters in "cat" as "cta," making it difficult to identify the word and determine the context in which it is being used. Math problems can be affected too. The equation *24 – 6* written on a smart board might look like *42 – 6* to a child with sequencing disabilities. In fact, they may get every answer wrong because they are seeing (and writing down) the math problem incorrectly.

Abstraction—the second part of integrating information—is the brain's ability to determine the correct meaning of a word or symbol. Individuals who have problems abstracting information may be unable to apply something they just read to a bigger, more general idea. For instance, they might be able to talk about a specific firefighter from a story, but they might find it difficult to relate this to the general idea of firefighters in their community. Even jokes can be hard to understand for individuals with abstraction disabilities.

Once the brain has made sense of the information, it is held in short-term memory. Memory is part of the brain's storage process. Information in short-term memory is held for only as long as it is concentrated on; an interruption in concentration means that the information is forgotten. For most people, remembering a phone number or the words on a spelling list is not too difficult. However, for those with learning disabilities, remembering these things may not be possible for them at all. Information that is not stored in a person's short-term memory cannot be transferred into their long-term memory, so instead of learning something and remembering it later, someone with a learning disability that affects their short-term memory may need to relearn certain things repeatedly.

In the final step of the learning process, the brain sends a message to the nerves and muscles to express the information as output. Output can take the form of writing, speaking, drawing, gesturing with the hands, or moving other muscles of the body. A learning disability that affects the output step might make it hard to communicate verbally or in writing. It might also interfere with the signals the brain sends to the muscles of the hand and fingers and make it difficult to form the letters of the alphabet.

To an outsider, children experiencing these problems might be seen as lazy, clumsy, or just not paying attention. This, of course, is completely untrue, and it is the reason why public awareness is the key to better education and support for these unique learners.

The Complexity of Learning

Inside the brain, the steps of the learning process do not look orderly at all. Learning is a complex process that involves billions of microscopic brain cells called neurons, the electrical signals they constantly relay back and forth to each other, and the hundreds of chemicals that either stimulate the cells to send signals or stop them from doing so.

A baby's brain is incredibly underdeveloped because it is designed to grow through learning. Until recently, neuroscientists believed that a baby's brain contains all of the neurons they will ever have. Ongoing research, however, is finding that the opposite may be true. According to the National Institute of Neurological Disorders and Stroke, "As children we might produce some new neurons to help build the pathways—called neural circuits—that act as information highways between different areas of the brain."[8]

As babies grow and take in sensory information from the outside world, neurons are activated and begin to branch out. This, in turn, stimulates these neurons to fire and send electrical charges to connect to other neurons, setting off a chain reaction until the message either reaches its destination or gets lost or interrupted along the way. The more a child practices and learns a new concept or skill, the stronger the connections, or synapses, between neurons become. The less a child uses a skill, the weaker the synapses will become. Essentially, this means that a child will learn through repetition and will forget a skill if it is not practiced enough.

Learning takes place throughout different parts of the brain, involving four lobes in two different

For children with learning disabilities, making new connections between neurons (shown here) does not always happen the way it should.

hemispheres. The frontal lobe is responsible for behavior while the left temporal and parietal lobes are responsible for reading—they help match sounds with letters. In a person with a learning disability, these lobes are often found to be less active than their peers', which is why reading and remembering words may be difficult for them. The cerebellum is responsible for large and fine motor function, such as tying shoes or walking, while both the right and left parietal lobes help with numbers and math. If a child is having difficulty in math, then these lobes may also appear to be underactive when compared to others'. The complexity of the brain means that learning is not a simple process. For those with learning disabilities, learning a new skill or concept can be incredibly difficult.

Using Their Brains

Beginning in the late 1970s, researchers started to use magnetic resonance imaging (MRI) technology to better understand the inner workings of people's bodies. MRI uses powerful magnetic fields and radio waves to detect changes in the protons of living tissue. These changes create a 3-D map of the area of the body being scanned. The MRI can then be compared to thousands of other scans to determine how it is similar to or different from a "typical" scan. MRIs are often used to examine injuries in the body, including the brain, with higher clarity compared to standard X-rays. In the late 1990s, researchers discovered that these MRIs could not only look at brain structure but brain functions as well.

Functional magnetic resonance imaging (fMRI) creates images that show which areas of the brain are active as a person carries out a task such as reading or writing. The way the scan works is relatively simple: When circuits of neurons are active, they consume more energy. This causes more blood to flow to the brain. The person being scanned is asked to perform a certain task, and as they do so, more blood flows into the parts of the brain required to complete that task. The fMRI scan detects where this increased blood flow is occurring, which appears as bright areas on the scan.

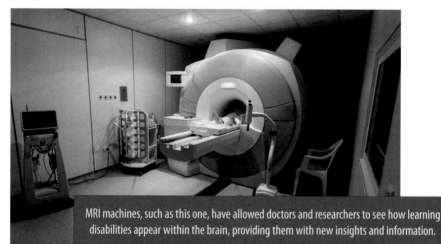

MRI machines, such as this one, have allowed doctors and researchers to see how learning disabilities appear within the brain, providing them with new insights and information.

In a 2015 study performed by the University of Washington, fMRIs were used to compare the white and gray matter in the brains of 40 children. Both gray and white matter are the areas in the brain where neurons branch out when learning occurs or a learned task is performed. Of these 40 children, 31 had been diagnosed with learning disabilities such as dyslexia and dysgraphia, both of which are related to spelling, reading, and handwriting. According to the University of Washington, "The children were asked to write the next letter in the alphabet following a letter they were shown, to write the missing letter in a word spelling, to rest without any task, and to plan a text about astronauts,"[9] using a special fiber-optic pen that was developed specifically for this study. The pen allowed researchers to record the children's writing and measure their brain function with fMRI at the same time.

The results demonstrated that the brains of children with learning disabilities worked less efficiently when performing these word-related tasks. Essentially, their brains had to work harder to think and process language when compared to the control group—the group without any diagnosed learning disabilities. Furthermore, the researchers also discovered that the brains of children with dyslexia and dysgraphia did not look alike, meaning that no two learning disabilities are the same—nor should they be treated as such. Currently, the term "learning disabilities" is used to describe all learning disabilities, despite the differences in how the children think and learn. Studies such as this one may encourage schools to provide more funding and education that is better tailored for each individual child.

Countless Causes

Brain-imaging studies can reveal where in the brain a learning disability occurs, but they do not explain the cause behind these brain changes. Scientists, doctors, and researchers believe that a variety of different factors can cause learning disabilities. Many people believe learning disabilities are at least partially genetic, or passed down from parents to children through genes, which control everything from eye color to the likelihood of developing certain diseases. One piece of evidence for the genetic theory is the study of learning disabilities in twins. Identical twins develop when a fertilized egg in a woman's womb splits into two. Each half becomes a whole person, and since they were once one, they have nearly identical DNA. Fraternal twins develop when two different eggs are fertilized at once. They are born at the same time, like identical twins, but they do not have identical DNA. Twin studies have been very useful in helping researchers get a better idea of what is determined by genes and what is determined by environmental factors. The National Association of Special Education Teachers found that "if one twin has a reading disability, the probability of the other twin also having a reading disability is 68 percent for identical twins ... and 40 percent for fraternal twins."[10]

Most researchers believe a combination of genetics and environmental factors contribute to learning disabilities. For example, children learn by modeling their parents' actions, so if a child has a parent with a learning disability, it is possible that they are learning and copying the behaviors and actions of the parent. Much evidence suggests that toxins in a child's environment, such as traces of lead in a child's home, are linked to developing learning disabilities as well. In the past, lead was used in paint and plumbing until it became clear how toxic it is to a child's developing brain. While it is no longer used in these household items today, old houses may still have them, so a child could accidentally eat lead paint chips or drink water from lead pipes.

Any damage to the brain, whether mild or severe, can create a variety of problems at any stage of a person's life. A child who sustains a head injury through play or a simple accident can sometimes develop a learning disability. Brain development can even be disrupted while a child is still in the womb from things such as premature birth, the mother's use of alcohol or drugs during the pregnancy, prolonged labor, lack of oxygen during birth, and even low birth weight.

The brain is meant to work in certain ways to process information and perform tasks. When its formation or development is damaged or hindered in any way, the brain has to find new ways to complete the same functions. The brain can actually "rewire" itself to allow it to learn new skills or relearn old ones. By rewiring itself, however, the brain sometimes has to work harder to complete the same tasks. In other cases, the brain may mix up simple information, making it difficult to complete simple word or math problems. It is for this reason that people with learning disabilities may find themselves working slower than their peers when it comes to math, writing, or reading. Individualized education programs in schools take these factors into account, creating a better schooling experience for those with learning disabilities.

Potential Bias

The National Center for Learning Disabilities estimates that 15 to 20 percent of Americans have a learning disability. These people belong to every race, ethnicity, and income level, and they are found in all regions of the country and the world. Approximately 5 percent of all school-enrolled children in the United States have some type of learning disability, and an estimated 4.6 million children have received an actual diagnosis. These numbers, however, are likely too low, as there are many factors that can delay a diagnosis. For example, a teacher may overlook a child's struggles in the classroom for too long, while another child's parents may be afraid to have their child "labeled" with a learning disability. The longer it takes to get a diagnosis, the longer it will take for that child to receive the help that they need—and deserve.

Many doctors and researchers agree that learning disabilities are the result of many different factors and can therefore affect anybody. According to Dr. Sheldon Horowitz, "Learning disabilities are NOT caused by economic disadvantage, environmental factors, or cultural differences. In fact, there is frequently no apparent cause for learning disabilities."[11] Despite this general agreement, The National Center for Learning Disabilities has found that children from low-income backgrounds are actually more likely to be diagnosed with a learning disability. Potential bias in research might be a factor, as one study determined that students from low-income backgrounds were being over-identified as having learning disabilities. Another factor might be the risks that poverty itself brings—such as increased lead exposure and chronic stress—that could later lead to signs of learning disabilities.

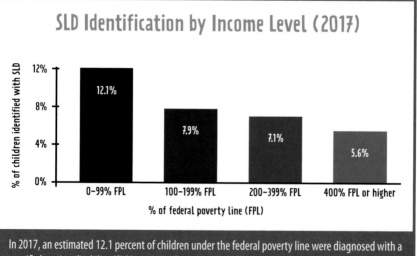

SLD Identification by Income Level (2017)

In 2017, an estimated 12.1 percent of children under the federal poverty line were diagnosed with a specific learning disability (SLD), as this information from the National Center on Learning Disorders shows. Bias may be part of the reason why that percentage decreases as income level increases.

Gender bias also plays a role in diagnosis. People tend to believe that boys are more likely to have learning disabilities than girls, and research shows that two-thirds of students with diagnosed learning disabilities are boys. However, studies are finding that there is no major difference between boys and girls when it comes to learning disabilities. So why, then, does this belief—and discrepancy in diagnosis—exist? A lot of it might come down to bias, as learning disability expert Bob Cunningham reported. He said, "One reason may be the differences in behaviors between boys and girls. We know that boys in general tend to draw more negative attention in schools. One report showed that boys represent around 85 percent of all discipline referrals. Another showed that 22 percent of boys had been formally disciplined, versus 8 percent of girls."[12]

Boys, therefore, are more likely to be identified with a learning disability because of something called referral bias. This means that because people expect boys to be more prone to learning disabilities, they are more likely to notice those behaviors in boys and refer them for help. However, this does not mean more boys than girls have learning disabilities; it simply means their disability is noticed more often. In contrast to how boys with learning disabilities and ADHD frequently behave—loud, disruptive, and calling attention to themselves—girls with these same disorders are more likely to be quiet, daydream or talk in class instead of paying attention, and they are more likely to show symptoms of anxiety or depression. As Cunningham explained, "their behavior appears more typical of how other girls behave,"[13] so their learning disability often goes unnoticed.

In 2014, the National Center for Learning Disabilities reported,

Research studies show that equal numbers of boys and girls share the most common characteristic of LD—difficulty with reading. Consequently, many girls with learning difficulties may go unidentified and unserved by special education … Two-thirds of students identified with LD are male (66 percent) while overall public school enrollment is almost evenly split between males (51 percent) and females (49 percent). This overrepresentation of boys occurs across different racial and ethnic groups.[14]

This report emphasizes the importance of education and continuing research in ensuring that boys and girls receive an equal amount of support in the classroom.

Unique Struggles

Not all children who struggle in school have a learning disability. Everyone learns and matures at a different rate. People also have different ways of learning. Some might study for a test by reading new vocabulary out loud, while others look at the words silently and commit them to memory. Some prefer to complete a long-term assignment by spreading the work out over several days, while others work more intensively and finish in one session. These are learning styles and preferences, but they are not learning disabilities. Children who grow up in poverty or in immigrant families where English is not spoken at home have fewer chances to develop their vocabularies in childhood. They often struggle to learn to read or write when they reach school age, and their teachers may incorrectly label them as "learning disabled." Being poor or disadvantaged can make it extremely challenging for students to achieve success in school, but it does not make these students learning disabled.

Sometimes the media and the public confuse

autism, Asperger's syndrome, and ADHD with learning disabilities. People with Asperger's and autism experience difficulty with language, emotions, and social skills—all of which can overlap with symptoms of learning disabilities. The symptoms of ADHD, too, can overlap with those of learning disabilities, such as staying focused or listening in the classroom. ADHD, however, is categorized differently by medical professionals; it is not classified as a specific learning disability.

For many years, people with learning disabilities were labeled "mentally retarded," which evolved into a hurtful label. In 2010, President Barack Obama signed Rosa's Law, which changed the term to "intellectually disabled" at the federal level. This does not mean it is illegal for regular citizens to use the term, although it

The Problem with the "R-Word"

Many people use what some call "the r-word" to describe not just people, but also objects and situations. It is common to hear people say "He's a retard" when someone makes a mistake or "That's so retarded" when something silly or confusing happens to them or a friend. Many do not understand what is wrong with the word, especially if they are not using it to describe a person. However, as the word has become an insult for people with intellectual disabilities, it is incredibly hurtful for people with these types of disabilities to hear—even if it is not directed at them specifically. As Ellen Seidman wrote in an article for the *Huffington Post*, "You wouldn't make fun of someone who was deaf or paralyzed—or use their disabilities as insults, would you? As in, you'd never say 'Oh, my boss is such a quadriplegic!'"[1]

The word is so hurtful that the Special Olympics started a campaign called Spread the Word to End the Word encouraging people to pledge to stop using the r-word completely. On its website, the organization noted, "when 'retard' and 'retarded' are used as synonyms for 'dumb' or 'stupid' by people without disabilities, it only reinforces stereotypes of people with intellectual disabilities being less valued members of humanity."[2] It may help people understand the hurtfulness of this word if they imagine it being replaced with something that describes them, such as their own name.

1. Ellen Seidman, "Quiz: Do You Get Why You Shouldn't Say the R-Word?," *Huffington Post*, March 6, 2013. www.huffingtonpost.com/ellen-seidman/do-you-get-why-you-shouldnt-say-the-r-word_b_2820595.html.

2. "Why Pledge," R-Word.org, accessed on October 15, 2018. www.r-word.org/r-word-why-pledge.aspx.

is considered offensive and rude; it simply means any law or policy that affects intellectually disabled people will use this more appropriate terminology.

Children who are intellectually disabled perform significantly below the average range on a test of intelligence. To meet the criteria for a learning disability, a child must demonstrate average or above average intellectual capacity even if they are achieving below-grade-level expectations. Although the terms sound similar, an intellectual disability is not a learning disability.

CHAPTER TWO

EXPLORING LEARNING DISABILITIES

There are many different labels used to describe the types of disabilities that interfere with learning. This can lead to confusion when professionals with different backgrounds and expertise use different terms to describe similar or overlapping conditions. For example, a teacher might describe a child who struggles to read and write as having dyslexia. A psychologist who evaluates the child's learning problems might call their condition a "language-based learning disability," while a speech and language therapist could determine that they have an "auditory processing deficit." Labels such as "dyslexia" (difficulty with reading) and "dyscalculia" (trouble with math) are widely used as a way of describing the challenges students face in academic subject areas, but learning disabilities rarely fit into neat academic categories.

Some children with dyslexia have no problem writing words, but they struggle with reading words. Other children can have two disabilities at once, where they struggle with both reading and writing words. Even one disability can make school and life challenging; with two, diagnosis becomes more difficult, creating the possibility that someone may not receive help for a few years. Thankfully, experts' understanding of the brain has evolved to provide some answers as to why these learning disabilities occur. This means that educators have begun to look beyond labels to ask where in the learning process a breakdown occurs in the brain—whether it is during input, storage, or output. People who understand the characteristics of learning disabilities can help provide better support and increase the self-esteem of those who have them.

Dyslexia

The word dyslexia comes from the Greek words *dys*, meaning "impaired," and *lexis*, meaning "word" or "language." "Dyslexia" is widely used to describe a learning disability that causes difficulty with reading, spelling, and writing. People with dyslexia struggle to recognize and decode written words; they read slowly and inaccurately and often have poor spelling. They may also skip words or entire lines of text and have difficulty staying focused on the material. Dyslexia is relatively common. A Yale University study on reading performance followed 445 students through their 12 years of school in the state of Connecticut. Researchers involved in that study estimated that one out of every five of the students showed some signs of dyslexia. Furthermore, they determined that dyslexia did not correlate with students' IQ levels. According to researcher Sally Shaywitz, "High-performing dyslexics are very intelligent, often out-of-the box thinkers and problem-solvers."[15]

For many years, researchers assumed that dyslexia was linked to problems in the way the brain processes visual information. This is because dyslexia is most often associated with what is called "mirror reading," where letters appear reversed or backwards. This, however, is a misconception. Researchers have found no evidence to suggest that people with dyslexia actually see words or letters backwards. In fact, many children write backwards early on because their brains are still learning the correct way to form letters and words. Instead, research on the brain has shown that dyslexia is linked to a breakdown in the auditory processing and sequencing phase of the learning process. People with dyslexia have trouble breaking down words into the smallest separate units of sound, called phonemes. Phonemes are what help people put sounds together to form words and connect the sounds to written letters. Educators call this group of skills "phonological awareness."

People with dyslexia also struggle to retrieve the sounds of letters and words from memory and apply this when they encounter new words or try to recall familiar words. When a child who is learning to read sees the letters *d-o-g*, for example, they retrieve the sounds for those letters from memory and then blend the sounds and read the word *dog*. Many of the same auditory-processing skills are crucial not only in reading but also in other areas of language learning. People who have dyslexia may have trouble with writing, spelling, memorizing and recalling vocabulary, following verbal instructions, or communicating clearly. Educators often use the term "language-based learning disabilities" to refer to all of these difficulties in receiving, processing,

Educators who know different ways of teaching reading skills are some of the best supports students with dyslexia can have.

and expressing written or oral language. People have been found to have dyslexia in every culture that has a written language, including languages that do not use the Roman alphabet (the one used in English and many other modern-day languages).

Despite the fact that dyslexia is a lifelong learning disability, children can still learn how to read if they have the right education and support from teachers and parents.

Dysgraphia

Dysgraphia, or difficulty with writing, also falls under language-based learning disabilities. According to Understood, an organization dedicated to helping the parents of children with learning disabilities, "The term comes from the Greek words *dys* ('impaired') and *graphia* ('making letter forms by hand'). Dysgraphia is a brain-based issue. It's not the result of a child being lazy."[16] Because dysgraphia makes it difficult to form and write letters, people who have it typically have messy handwriting that is hard to read.

Like reading, writing is a complicated process. Dysgraphia can be caused by a breakdown during one or more of the steps of learning, including processing and sequencing, memory, or output and expression. People who have difficulty sequencing and organizing auditory information, including those with dyslexia, may find it difficult to recall the order of letters and words as they write and need to slow down to write correctly. Others may experience extreme difficulty with the mechanics of spelling and punctuation. When dysgraphia is linked to fine motor output or expression, there is a problem in the way the brain relays messages to coordinate the muscles of the dominant hand (the one the person feels most comfortable writing with).

Strategies for Success

Because writing is such an important part of school, people who have dysgraphia may find simple things such as note-taking to be incredibly frustrating. Furthermore, if their handwriting on homework and tests looks sloppy, they may find themselves having to redo their work or clarify their answers. Word processors, assistant note-takers, audio recording, and pre-printed worksheets are good places to start, but there are other tools and accommodations that exist to help these students succeed. For example, specialized pencil grips help students with dysgraphia hold pens and pencils correctly. This allows for more controlled and accurate writing. Additionally, raised paper, which has textured lines, provides sensory cues to the student's brain.

Sensory cues are helpful because they give students a guide to help them stay within lines and form letters correctly as they write. Highlighted lined paper provides visual cues to guide children in creating properly sized letters, while slanted writing boards make the physical process of writing more comfortable. Many schools are also turning to apps on tablets and computers in the classroom. Some apps take digital photos of worksheets and allow students to write in and complete their answers on the screen. Others provide the option to physically trace letters on the screen, helping these students learn letters by building muscle memory through repetition. Over time, the muscles in the hand "remember" how to make the letters—even if the brain does not—because they have done it so many times. Although dysgraphia can be difficult to live with, a person's level of stress and discomfort can be greatly diminished using any combination of these tools.

Tablets are incredibly helpful for visual learners, and add-ons such as tactile screens can further improve their learning. These textured, removable screens provide sensory input as children with learning disorders trace letters and numbers, helping to build their muscle memory.

People who have dysgraphia often complain that their hands cannot work as fast as their minds are thinking. Even filling in the blanks on a school form or job application with information the person knows well, such as name and address, can turn into a tedious process. Some people with dysgraphia also have trouble with written expression. They become so stressed during the physical process of writing that they lose hold of the messages and ideas they want to express. They often describe staring hopelessly at a blank page for minutes or even hours, unable to let their ideas stream from their heads onto the paper. In many cases, typing on a computer keyboard allows them to express themselves more freely and effectively.

Dyspraxia

Some people with dysgraphia also struggle with the mechanics of writing because they cannot make the muscles in their dominant hand work together. This is a fine motor disability, also referred to as developmental coordination disorder or dyspraxia, from the Greek word *praxia*, meaning "movement." It can interfere with any tasks that involve the coordination of groups of fine, or small, muscles, including cutting with scissors, tying shoes, coloring within the lines of a drawing, buttoning a shirt, or typing. People with dyspraxia have to concentrate on the movements their fingers and hands are making while they are writing, cutting, or drawing to effectively complete such a task. Sometimes dyspraxia affects gross motor skills, or the coordination of larger muscle groups. People who have a gross motor disability often appear clumsy and bump into things or have trouble with physical activities such as running or climbing. Activities that require hand-eye coordination, such as hitting a baseball with a bat, can be difficult to accomplish. As adults, they may struggle with routine tasks such as driving, cooking, or shaving. In some cases, dyspraxia interferes with the ability to speak because the areas of the brain that control hand and mouth movements are close together in the brain's central cortex.

A child with dyspraxia may have a difficult time learning how to use scissors, writing their name, and putting on clothes.

As of 2019, it is estimated that 6 to 10 percent of children suffer from dyspraxia. Children with dyspraxia may find it difficult to do things such as color, assemble puzzles, and even play with classmates outside. This can seriously affect the child's self-esteem. During early childhood, it is believed that some children with dyspraxia skip the crawling stage completely, and they master skills such as standing, walking, and talking slower than their peers. Although dyspraxia largely affects a person's motor skills, it can also have an effect on social skills as well. This is because, according to Understood, "They can have trouble pronouncing words or expressing their ideas. They may also have trouble adjusting the pitch and volume of their voice."[17] This can affect how they make friends because they may appear to be yelling at someone when they do not mean to.

While dyspraxia can cause learning problems in children, it has nothing to do with their intelligence. Highly intelligent children with dyspraxia may appear to be more immature when compared to their peers because their motor difficulties tend to make them self-conscious and anxious when they are in groups. Speech, occupational, and physical therapies can all be used to lessen the effects of dyspraxia.

Researchers believe that both fine and gross motor disabilities are most often caused by a problem in the output phase of the learning process. In order to run, jump, or write, the brain has to send messages to the nerves and muscles to complete the action. A motor disability may also involve visual-spatial processing. In this case, the person processes visual

Types of Dyspraxia

Because dyspraxia can affect different areas of the body and their related movements, it can be broken down into smaller categories.

- **Oromotor dyspraxia:** Also known as apraxia of speech, this type of dyspraxia makes the formation of words difficult. When muscles cannot be coordinated well enough to pronounce words, speech may come out slurred, slow, and hard to understand.

- **Ideomotor dyspraxia:** This type makes it difficult to perform single motor tasks. These are simple movements such as waving hello, brushing hair, or chewing food.

- **Ideational dyspraxia:** Ideational dyspraxia relates to multi-motor tasks, or anything that has to be done in a sequence. This includes things such as cooking, bathing, driving, or making a bed.

- **Dressing dyspraxia:** This form of dyspraxia affects a person's sense of orientation of their clothing—upright, backwards, etc. Their sequence of dressing is impaired as well, making getting dressed very difficult.

- **Constructional dyspraxia:** This type of dyspraxia relates to a person's perception of spatial relationships. Therefore, it is difficult to build with blocks, copy drawings accurately, or work with geometric drawings.

or spatial information poorly and relays information to the muscles incorrectly during activities such as catching a ball or jumping rope.

Dyscalculia

Dyscalculia, or difficulty with math, causes difficulty solving math problems and grasping numerical relationships. Students may have trouble understanding the meaning of numbers and their written equivalent. For instance, they may not realize that the number 10 is actually the same thing as the word "ten," or they may have a sequencing issue and have trouble organizing the information required to solve a math problem. They may also struggle with the language of math or have short-term memory problems that prevent them from memorizing and retrieving math facts and formulas. Researchers believe that math disabilities are nearly as common as language-based disabilities, but they often go undetected. In most schools, students must fall far behind their classmates in math before they are diagnosed with a learning disability. This is because many non-learning-disabled students struggle with one or more aspects

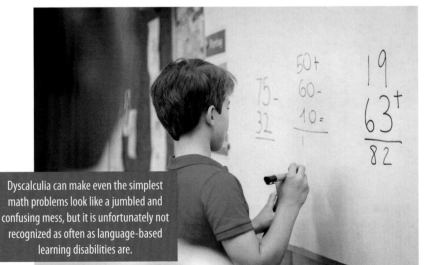

Dyscalculia can make even the simplest math problems look like a jumbled and confusing mess, but it is unfortunately not recognized as often as language-based learning disabilities are.

of math too. Many also develop math phobias because of a negative experience in a math class or a lack of self-confidence. This makes it harder to recognize when a child's math problems stem from a disability.

Dyscalculia is even more complicated because it often occurs alongside other learning disorders. Reading disabilities such as dyslexia are believed to appear in 43 to 65 percent of children who also suffer from dyscalculia. This math-related learning disability is also sometimes tied to a handful of genetic disorders as well as intense anxiety. When a child becomes too nervous in school, their performance suffers. Math anxiety affects many children, and its effects are magnified when coupled with dyscalculia.

NVLD

While dyscalculia can be caused by a breakdown in visual-processing skills, people with a nonverbal learning disability (NVLD) have a more widespread visual- and spatial-processing weakness. NVLDs, however, do not affect a person's language skills such as speaking and writing. In fact, their language skills tend to be strong. Instead, NVLDs affect social skills—things such as detecting sarcasm and staying on topic during a conversation. It is for this reason that people with NVLDs tend to be awkward in social situations. They frequently fail to interpret nonverbal cues such as facial expressions, gestures, and body language, and they can misread important social cues that make it harder to make and maintain friendships. Living with an NVLD means that a person can sometimes take language too literally as well as share some information at inappropriate times. Physically, they tend to appear uncoordinated, and during conversation, they might stand too close to the person they are talking to.

NVLDs affect not only a person's social life but their academic life as well. Children with an NVLD may be able to read an entire story but be unable to tell somebody the story's main theme. Math-related word problems are difficult to complete because comprehension skills are lacking. Unfortunately, some parents and teachers may see these issues and think the child is being inattentive or lazy. Researchers continue to look into the reasons behind NVLDs, and its status as a recognized disability is still up for debate. Currently, it is believed that NVLDs occur because of the way information is processed between the left and right hemispheres of the brain.

It is important to note that Asperger's syndrome, which is a mild form of autism, has very similar symptoms to NVLDs. In fact, an estimated 80 percent of children with NVLD symptoms also have Asperger's. As with any learning disability, with the right tools and support, children with NVLDs can learn to cope with their symptoms.

From the Simple to the Complex

Both nonverbal and language-based learning disabilities are often accompanied by a weakness in executive function. According to the LDA, "executive functioning affects planning, organization, strategizing, attention to details and managing time and space."[18] This term is used to describe the set of mental processes that people use to regulate behaviors and accomplish a task.

Executive function can be compared to the conductor of an orchestra or the coach of a sports team. They oversee everything to ensure that actions are being performed accurately and effectively. When that direction becomes weak, so does the quality of the tasks being carried out. Executive function allows people to perform simple tasks, such as throwing a ball or picking up a pencil, as well as the more complex, such as planning for a party or studying and memorizing skills for an exam. It even has a hand in regulating emotions and attentiveness.

People who have a learning disability as well as executive function weakness struggle to stay organized and carry out tasks in a timely and efficient way. They may have trouble starting a project or estimating how long it will take. They may find it difficult to come up with ideas independently or to tell a story from start to finish without getting lost in the details. They often lack motivation to finish a task, especially when it seems difficult or frustrating. They may also struggle to retain information in working memory for long enough to make use of it.

The idea of executive function is widely used and accepted by researchers, but it is more of a theory than something that is easily measured or defined. Researchers believe that as the brain matures and forms new learning connections, executive function changes and develops too. This process can be improved when children are directly taught to organize, plan, and monitor their own behaviors.

Closely Linked, but Not the Same

ADHD is a behavioral condition that is closely linked to learning disabilities. According to the LDA,

> *ADHD is not considered to be a learning disability. It can be determined to be a disability under the Individuals with Disabilities Education Act (IDEA), making a student eligible to receive special education services. However, ADHD falls under the "Other Health Impaired" category and not under "Specific Learning Disabilities."*[19]

Despite not being a learning disability, ADHD still

can have major effects on those who do have learning disabilities. ADHD is seen in an estimated 2 million children in the United States, and 20 to 30 percent of children with ADHD also have a diagnosed learning disability. Children with ADHD tend to act impulsively, fidget in their seats, and talk nearly nonstop. These behaviors in the classroom are hard to ignore. A subset of ADHD called attention deficit disorder (ADD) causes the same difficulty with attention that ADHD does, but people with ADD lack the "hyperactivity" component. These children tend to daydream and zone out, but they do not display the energetic hyperactivity that makes ADHD behaviors disruptive.

The Centers for Disease Control and Prevention (CDC) states that ADHD "is a serious public health problem affecting a large number of children and adults."[20] Research has found that mentions of children with symptoms of ADHD actually appear in literature dating all the way back to the 19th century. Experts believe Sir Arthur Crichton, a Scottish doctor who treated adult patients whose symptoms included difficulty concentrating and emotional outbursts, may have first described it in scientific literature in 1763. ADHD, therefore, is not a recent health problem. What is recent, however, is the understanding behind it—understanding that researchers, scientists, doctors, and even teachers can use to better support those living with ADHD, including those who show signs of both ADHD and one or more learning disabilities.

Emotional and Behavioral Problems

Even when ADHD is not a factor, learning disabilities and behavioral or emotional problems are often linked. Students with a learning disability generally have to work harder to succeed than their peers and tend to receive more negative feedback from teachers and classmates. When rated by their peers and teachers, they are often seen as behaving in less socially acceptable ways than other students. Many exhibit emotional and behavioral problems that grow out of their frustrations and anxieties as they struggle to learn and to fit in with their classmates. Many young people find it preferable to attract attention as the class clown who always makes other students laugh by acting out than to be singled out in school for daydreaming or having poor grades because of their learning disability.

Undiagnosed or unaddressed learning disorders can cause students to feel frustrated, embarrassed, and unintelligent. This is why identifying them early in life is so important.

Low expectations and low self-esteem take a heavy toll on many children with learning disabilities. By the time they enter high school, many have experienced so much failure that some will reject the school environment altogether. In the 2013 to 2014 school year, it was estimated that students with learning disabilities were almost three times more likely to drop out of high school than their peers. They have also been shown to be far more likely to turn to drugs and alcohol to cope with their frustrations or to get into trouble with the law and end up in the juvenile justice system. As adults, they are twice as likely to be unemployed. For many with learning disabilities, unaddressed emotional problems such as anger, frustration, and low self-esteem are often as much of a barrier to success as their academic weaknesses.

CHAPTER THREE

FROM "WORD-BLIND" TO "DYSLEXIC"

From the earliest days of public education, children with learning disabilities have suffered misunderstanding and mistreatment in schools. For decades, they were labeled brain-damaged, mentally retarded, lazy, or unmotivated. To make matters worse, they were punished, humiliated, and bullied by teachers and classmates. Until the 1970s, they were likely to be separated from their peers and placed in isolated classrooms with children who were intellectually or physically disabled or who had severe behavioral and emotional problems. It was not uncommon for a child with a learning disability to be held back in school for multiple years. Most never graduated from high school or dreamed of pursuing a college degree.

Researchers studied children and adults with reading and writing difficulties as early as the 19th century and published their findings in scientific and professional journals. In 1877, a German neurologist by the name of Adolph Kussmaul created the term "word-blind." This was a term meant to describe patients who were unable to read despite strong intellectual capabilities in speaking and other aspects. In 1887, the public saw the term "dyslexia" used for the first time by German physician Rudolf Berlin. For the next couple of decades, other studies began to focus on learning disabilities in students. Researchers tried to develop new methods of instruction to support children with learning difficulties, but their efforts had little lasting impact.

The world's understanding of learning disabilities today is much different than it was 100 years ago. In 1909, students with learning disabilities did not have the same legal protections or quality of education that is provided to students today.

In the 1960s and 1970s, life for people with learning disabilities finally began to change for the better. Inspired by the civil rights movement, which aimed to make life better for black people in America, a growing disability rights movement began to take shape. The Anti-Defamation League (ADL) explained, "The struggle for disability rights has followed a similar pattern to many other civil rights movements—challenging negative attitudes and stereotypes, rallying for political and institutional change, and lobbying for the self-determination of a minority community."[21] In April 1963, a conference was held in Chicago, Illinois, by the parents of children with various disabilities. As the LDA described it, "professionals and parents shared a common concern: the recognition of the dire need for services for their children, services that did not exist."[22]

In response to these actions, the U.S. government began to pass new laws and policies to protect people with learning disabilities from discrimination in schools, jobs, housing, and other areas of life. Over many years, public attitudes slowly began to change too.

An Evolution in Understanding

Learning disabilities first came to public attention in Europe in the late 19th century, when physicians began publishing accounts of their cases in medical journals. In December 1895, Scottish eye surgeon James Hinshelwood published an article about clinical cases of "word blindness," which would later become known as dyslexia. Like many researchers of the time, Hinshelwood originally assumed that dyslexia was linked to impaired or damaged visual perception. In published articles that followed over the years, Hinshelwood suggested changes in teaching practices that might best suit children who were diagnosed with the condition.

As research progressed, the way dyslexia was understood and treated changed. Samuel Orton was one of the key figures to advance understanding of reading and language disabilities, and his work spanned more than two decades, beginning in 1925. Orton was a neuropathologist—a doctor who specializes in problems of the nervous system—who worked at the Greene County Mental Clinic in Iowa. Initially, he studied language problems in the mentally handicapped patients of that facility. Later on, Orton studied nearly 3,000 children and adults with language disabilities at the Neurological Institute of New York as well as at Columbia University. His research determined that learning disabilities were likely passed down from parents to children through genes, which determine many of a person's physical and mental traits. At the time, however, the inner workings of the brain were not well understood.

Orton attributed the children's difficulties to what he called a "lack of cerebral dominance," or the failure of one hemisphere of the brain to establish dominance over the other. He also developed a theory that explained why some children would see letters reversed in words. As research and science evolved, some of Orton's theories were eventually disproved. His work, however, inspired his wife and his colleague to continue their studies even after his death. The Orton Society was formed in 1949. This organization continues its work to this day as the International Dyslexia Association (IDA), improving the quality of life for people with learning disabilities and increasing the public's understanding of dyslexia.

America's Newest Pioneers

Orton was one of many researchers who played an important role in developing reading instruction for children with dyslexia. He was one of the first to advocate the step-by-step teaching of phonics, or letter-sound relationships, to children who had trouble learning to read. A popular method for teaching reading at the time was the look-say method, or reading by sight. By the mid-1950s, this teaching method was being criticized and debated as educators' views changed. Orton, along with others such as Anna Gillingham, Bessie Stillman, and Grace Fernald, pioneered new methods of reading instruction to help struggling readers.

At a time when other areas of research and science were often closed to them, women were making key contributions to the field of education. They designed new methods of reading instruction, many of which are still in use today. One example is called the Orton-Gillingham approach. It was specifically tailored to help children with reading difficulties by breaking reading and spelling down into smaller sets of skills that could be mastered and added onto over time.

Orton and Gillingham also pioneered the "multisensory" approach to reading. This includes the practice of three things at once: visual skills, auditory skills, and kinesthetic (movement-based) skills. Students speak words out loud, write words as they read them, and trace the letters with their fingers as they speak them—improving the connections they make to language and reading. Throughout the 1970s, progressive new theories changed the way teachers thought about teaching reading. Today, however, parents and social media are the newest pioneers. As the IDA stated, "Parent movements leveraging social media drive public policy and [are] increasing demand for trained teachers."[23]

The Danger of Negative Labels

Even though advances in reading instruction were made early on, learning disabilities were still not well understood. In the early 1940s, a new theory emerged to explain why some children who seemed intelligent might struggle to learn basic skills. Researchers observed that these children exhibited similar behaviors to people who had suffered brain damage, leading them to the conclusion that the children, therefore, must have a little bit of brain damage as well. The theory of minimal brain damage died in the 1960s after observations and testing failed to show any evidence for it. Researchers then revised their thinking and proposed instead that children's learning difficulties must stem from problems with brain functioning. The term "minimal brain damage" was replaced by "minimal brain dysfunction syndrome," with the word "dysfunction" included to suggest that these children's brains were impaired in some way.

This new theory came much closer to describing the differences in connections between neurons that scientists would observe in people with learning disabilities many years later using advanced imaging technologies such as magnetic resonance imaging (MRI). However, the label "minimal brain dysfunction," like "minimal brain damage," reinforced negative stereotypes and implied that people with learning disabilities were defective or broken. For decades, these labels influenced the way teachers, parents, and classmates viewed children with learning disabilities. They also had a profoundly negative effect on the way the children saw themselves. Unfortunately, these stereotypes and negative views, also known as stigmas, still exist. New studies and programs are aimed at creating classroom education that is universal, where children with learning disabilities can be taught in the same way their peers are to remove any negative stigmas.

Labels and stereotypes have negative and lasting effects that have been proven to affect academic performance in the classroom. One person working to change this is Gabrielle Rappolt-Schlichtmann, co-president of a nonprofit organization called CAST, which is aiming to create a Universal Design for Learning in classrooms. Her story makes her work with CAST a very personal one. In an interview for Harvard University, she said,

> *One of the reasons that I do this work is that I'm dyslexic and I experienced stigmatization and stereotype threat all the way through school. Reflecting back on it, I think having a label changed how other people perceived my ability to be successful in school. So, I would say from my personal experience: You are not alone; you are not broken; you can be successful.*[24]

The Father of Special Education

As early as the 1930s, there were some people in the research and education communities who rejected labels such as "minimally brain damaged" and "mentally retarded," and who challenged the common practice of separating children with learning difficulties from their peers. For years, they were lone voices calling for change—until the evidence in support of their views could no longer be ignored. Some researchers questioned whether it was valid to use a single IQ test to measure intelligence and label children. Samuel Kirk, who is sometimes called the "Father of Special Education," was one of these critics. Kirk was a respected psychologist who strongly objected to the practice of labeling and defining students with terms such as "mentally retarded" and "dyslexic." He believed these labels created lowered expectations and limited children's potential for success in school and in life.

Despite his dislike for such labels, Kirk actually created a new label—learning disabled—to describe children who struggled to learn basic skills. This term had such power and impact that it forever

Why Do People Need Special Accommodations?

Many people believe that giving someone special accommodations for their learning disability is unfair to their peers who do not have a disability. They say that things such as getting extra time on a test or being allowed to type instead of handwrite their work give these students an unfair advantage over their classmates. Some people believe that students lie about having a disability in order to "cheat the system" and get these advantages.

In reality, educators carefully observe people who are believed to have a learning disability and can see them struggling with their work in ways their classmates do not. This is why someone must have a diagnosed, verifiable learning disability to qualify for special accommodations—to ensure that they do not "cheat the system." According to Ferris State University, when accommodations are based on the student's specific limitations, "they simply compensate for the aforementioned limitation, and therefore are not advantageous."[1] For example, if it takes them a long time to read the questions correctly, they may not finish the test when everyone else does, so an hour and a half of test-taking time may give someone with a learning disability the same amount of time to finish reading all the questions as an hour would for everyone else. Studies on this subject have shown that the grades of students without learning disabilities do not improve noticeably when given extra time, while the grades of students with learning disabilities do improve drastically.

1. "Do Accommodations Give Students with Learning Disabilities an Unfair Advantage?," Ferris State University, accessed on October 24, 2018. ferris.edu/HTMLS/colleges/university/disability/faculty-staff/FAQ/unfair.htm.

changed the special education field.

As a child, Kirk taught illiterate men working on his father's farm how to read. This work had a lasting and inspiring effect on the young boy, leading to a career working with people who had been labeled "mentally disabled." On April 6, 1963, Kirk spoke at the conference in Chicago held by parents who recognized that their children needed special education in order to succeed academically. During his speech, he used the term "learning disability" for the first time. The parents at the conference accepted this new term and, in the months that followed, they and other parents helped form the Association for Children with Learning Disabilities, which is known today as the Learning Disabilities Association of America (LDA). Dr. Kirk's work, however, was far from finished.

According to the Illinois Distributed Museum, "After his famous 1963 'learning disabilities' speech he was appointed by President John F. Kennedy to the post of Director of the Office of Education's Division of Handicapped Children for 1963 and 1964. During this time he convinced the government to provide money to train teachers of students with learning disabilities."[25] Kirk died in 1996 at the age of 92, but his work continues to inspire better education, more inclusive laws, and improved school programs to better assist those with learning disabilities. It is this kind of advocacy that improves the educational opportunities and the lives of people with learning disabilities around the globe.

A Dangerous and Damaging Trend

The broadening of the term "disability" to include learning disabilities created demand for support services in schools, but it was also sometimes used in unethical ways. In 1954, the U.S. Supreme Court ruled in a historic case, *Brown v. Board of Education*, that state laws establishing separate public schools for black and white students were unconstitutional. This was an era of deep-rooted racism, and parents and teachers in many school districts reacted to the decision with shock. They feared that white families would flee urban school districts and move to the suburbs if schools became racially integrated. Some schools, however, came up with a way to follow the ruling while still managing to keep black and white students segregated. Their idea was to increase the use of IQ testing to place students into separate classrooms.

In Washington, D.C., enrollment doubled in special education classes in 1955. Of the students enrolled in these classes, more than 75 percent were African American, and most of them were wrongly labeled either intellectually disabled or emotionally disturbed. Trends such as these still exist in American schools. In a 2010 study from the University of Texas, researchers reported, "The fact that disproportional identification with a learning disability occurs among groups who are already socially disadvantaged—racial/ethnic minorities, language minorities, students of low socioeconomic status (SES)—is of particular concern to both educators and researchers."[26] Male students were also found to be more likely to be labeled learning disabled.

The fact that disproportionate numbers exist in studies such as this one is very troubling. For one, some children may be incorrectly diagnosed based on gender and racial factors instead of the symptoms they display. Aside from the problems this causes for the misdiagnosed child, it creates a strong possibility that other children—the ones who truly do have a learning disability—are not getting the services and support they need as resources are being used elsewhere. Studies such as the one by the University of Texas help raise awareness that may lead to new and better ways of identifying and supporting learning disabilities in the classroom. In doing so, all children, regardless of background, may someday have an equal chance of receiving the support they need to succeed academically.

Problems with IQ Testing

Alfred Binet, a French psychologist, created the first IQ test in 1905. At the request of the French government, Binet came up with a way to determine which students would have the most academic difficulties in school. Binet, along with his colleague Théodore Simon, created a formula for calculating a child's mental age in comparison with their chronological age and called it an intelligence quotient, or IQ. The IQ scores were determined by asking the children questions regarding memory, problem solving, and attention skills.

In the United States, the Stanford-Binet IQ test first gained acceptance in 1916 when Lewis Terman, a psychologist at Stanford University, standardized the French test for American test-takers. In 1917, U.S. Army psychologists developed both written and picture-based IQ tests for more than 2 million World War I recruits. These tests were used to determine which positions were best suited for each recruit. In 1939, Romanian-American psychologist David Wechsler developed new versions of the test designed for children of various ages.

Because no alternative forms of screening for learning disabilities existed, IQ tests remained in schools for generations despite the fact that they had been proven ineffective in diagnosing these issues, as there is no link between intelligence and learning disabilities. In 2004, The American Psychological Association explained, "learning-disabled children often show normal or above average intelligence on IQ tests, but fail to achieve academically."[1] That same year, President George W. Bush revised the Individuals with Disabilities Education Act (IDEA) to remove the IQ testing requirement for children with learning disabilities.

1. Karen Kersting, "Debating Learning-Disability Identification," American Psychological Association, October 2004. www.apa.org/monitor/oct04/learningdisabil.aspx.

The Fight Continues

Disability rights movements have a long history, with some activist movements dating back to the 1800s. In the 1930s and 1940s, President Franklin D. Roosevelt, who was paralyzed from the waist down, worked to improve disability rights—but in those years, people believed disabilities should be hidden from the public eye. In fact, Roosevelt himself tried as hard as he could never to be photographed in his wheelchair. Smaller movements continued in America until the 1960s, when the major framework for disability rights caught the public eye and spurred more widespread changes. Inspired by the civil rights and women's liberation movements, disability rights groups formed across the nation to help create new policies, laws, and special education. The movement started with efforts to protect the rights of the intellectually disabled but quickly spread to those with a wide range of disabilities, from cerebral palsy to hearing impairment.

People with learning disabilities joined the larger movement for disability rights in 1963, when a group of concerned parents whose children struggled to read called a meeting in Chicago. The parents argued that their children had nothing wrong intellectually; furthermore, they knew that the labels placed on their children were damaging to their children's self-esteem. Samuel Kirk attended the meeting and delivered the speech in which he introduced the parents to the term "learning disability." According to the Anti-Defamation League, "Parent advocates were at the forefront, demanding that their children be taken out of institutions and asylums, and placed into schools where their children could have the opportunity to engage in society just like children who were not disabled."[27]

Educators slowly began to respond to the parents' demands. In schools across the country, special education services started to expand. In some districts, schools began to "mainstream" students with mild to moderate learning disabilities into general education classrooms for a greater portion of the school day, while also offering them support in special education resource rooms. Despite this progress, schools at this time were still under no legal obligation to provide services for students with learning disabilities, and the quality of special education programs differed across America. In the 1970s, courts found exclusion of disabled children in schools to be unconstitutional. Today, students are offered many more rights and opportunities thanks to better laws and policies.

The Spark of an IDEA

In 1975, the disability rights movement achieved a historic victory when the U.S. Congress passed Public Law 94-142, known at the time as the Education for All Handicapped Children Act. One of the purposes of this law was "to assure that all children with disabilities have available to them … a free appropriate public education which emphasizes special education and related services designed to meet their unique needs."[28] Children identified as having learning and other disabilities were to be mainstreamed into general education classrooms, and once there, they were also entitled to receive support services from trained resource specialists assigned to each school.

The 1975 law was a huge step in reversing decades of mistreatment, but it was an ambitious law that put a big strain on the resources of many schools. The government had vastly underestimated the number of children who would be identified as having learning disabilities as well as the expenses of evaluating and providing special education services for them. Schools simply became overwhelmed by the demand. Many teachers were unprepared for the changes and did little to modify their instruction for the students with disabilities who joined their classes. For years, parent and teacher groups complained

Beginning in 1975, students with various physical and mental disabilities were legally entitled to special education programs. Many schools have adopted inclusion classrooms in which these children can be in a classroom with their nondisabled peers.

about the lack of skilled teachers and instruction for disabled students. In 1980, a federal report proved that these parents were right. The report examined how schools had responded to the 1975 law. While

The Mainstreaming Law

The passage of the Education for All Handicapped Children Act, later renamed the Individuals with Disabilities Education Act (IDEA), set the stage for dramatic changes in public education. Before the law was passed, fewer than half of all U.S. children with known disabilities received a public or private school education. The law opened doors to children who had been barred by state laws from attending school. It also improved the quality of education for children with disabilities who were already part of the public school system. This included children with learning disabilities, who had been mistreated or isolated in special education classrooms for decades.

IDEA requires free and appropriate public education, or FAPE, for every child, regardless of their disability. This means that individualized education for disabled children costs nothing for their parents. The child's individualized education program (IEP) begins with an evaluation by a team of professionals and allows for input from the child's parents or caregivers. IDEA is sometimes called the "mainstreaming law" because it requires that children with disabilities be educated alongside their peers in the environment that puts the least restrictions on them. For some children with disabilities, IDEA has allowed them to become part of a regular classroom environment for the first time.

some children no doubt benefited from the law, an overwhelming majority were actually not much better off than before. Segregation of children with disabilities was still occurring, and those with learning disabilities were falling behind their peers and growing discouraged. In 1990, the U.S. Congress expanded and revised the 1975 law and renamed it the Individuals with Disabilities Education Act (IDEA). IDEA provided states with more federal funding and resources for special education, and today, it continues to protect students with all kinds of disabilities from discrimination in the classroom.

In many schools, mainstreaming is slowly being replaced by the idea of "inclusion," a teaching approach in which students with learning disabilities spend their entire school day in a general education classroom with both a general education teacher and a special education teacher. In inclusion classrooms, students with disabilities participate in all of the day's lessons and activities. Another law, known as the Americans with Disabilities Act (ADA), ensures that children and adults with learning disabilities face no discrimination in schools, workplaces, housing, or any other services open to the public. These laws and policies have enhanced the quality of life and access to education for tens of millions of children and adults with learning disabilities.

Many schools today have therapists and specially designed materials that allow children with learning disabilities to learn in a way that best meets their individual needs.

CHAPTER FOUR

THE KEY QUESTION

Since the passage of what is known today as IDEA, U.S. schools have made great strides away from the days when students were excluded or bullied for their academic difficulties. Many schools teach children to be tolerant and respectful of people who look, act, or learn differently. Special accommodations and inclusion classrooms are more widely available today than ever before.

Despite all of these advancements, for many students with learning disabilities, school remains a difficult place to learn. IDEA ensured that they would be educated alongside their nondisabled peers, but the law does not always result in better learning experiences or full inclusion in the school community. When President Gerald Ford signed the law, he recognized that it had issues, saying, "Everyone can agree with the objective stated in the title of this bill— educating all handicapped children in our Nation. The key question is whether the

President Gerald Ford initially wondered if IDEA would make an impact. Despite the lack of adequate government funding that still exists to this day, IDEA has managed to affect many children's lives in positive and meaningful ways.

bill will really accomplish that objective."[29] However, Ford also recognized the law's potential. After signing it, Ford spoke about working to "design a program which will recognize the proper Federal role in helping States and localities fulfill their responsibilities in educating handicapped children."[30]

Imperfect Abilities

The special education process in schools generally begins when teachers observe that a student is struggling and falling behind their classmates. However, even at this point, identifying children with legally recognized learning disabilities is rarely easy or straightforward. In 1977, the U.S. Office of Education defined a specific learning disability (SLD) as "a disorder in one or more of the basic psychological processes involved in understanding or in using language, spoken or written, which may manifest itself in an imperfect ability to listen, think, speak, read, write, spell, or to do mathematical calculations."[31] This wording also appears in IDEA as the federal definition of SLDs.

The phrase "imperfect ability" could apply to almost anyone who struggles with spelling, math, or reading. Teachers, however, have to use their professional skills and judgment to filter out students who are having these problems because of a learning disability. These disabilities are often found when a child reaches a certain grade where specific skills and topics are the focus. However, the earlier a child is recognized as having a learning disability, the sooner they can get an education that is specifically tailored to their needs and allows for the mastery of new and important academic skills. This, in turn, increases their chances of being successful in school and life later on.

Unfortunately, there are many students with learning disabilities who are misdiagnosed or never identified. Some children hide their struggles from teachers, family members, and friends out of embarrassment. Some will withdraw or sit quietly without disturbing the class until they become frustrated and unhappy. Others, who are active and involved, manage to get by with average work that teachers see as lazy and careless. As the LDA noted, children with learning disabilities "tend to withdraw or act out when a task is too demanding."[32]

The same behaviors can occur with students whose first language is not English; for them, reading can be a struggle because they lack experience decoding and reading English letters and words. Additionally, students in low-income schools may also display symptoms of a learning disability when they are just frustrated and confused. This is because in wealthier school districts, children are likely to have access to more books and highly skilled teachers. Students in these districts have been found to develop academic skills faster than those in lower-income environments. In America, a gap between the wealthy and impoverished still exists and creates unequal experiences for students in a variety of damaging ways. Learning disabilities—both in the way they are identified and handled—are no exception.

Researchers warn that failing to identify students with learning disabilities is extremely troubling because early intervention—as early as before kindergarten—can often make school much easier for them. In recent years, schools have begun adopting what is called a response to intervention (RTI) approach. In schools that use the RTI approach, all kindergarten children receive a universal screening to measure their skills. Working in small groups, teachers begin interacting with students and identify those who are at risk for learning difficulties. The classroom teacher first tries different approaches to the material. If the student does

How Learning Disabilities Appear in School

Research has shown that individualized special education has its greatest effect during a student's earliest years in school. While screening and services continue to improve for children with learning disabilities, there are many reasons why some of them fall behind. Lack of resources, individual student behavior, and quality of trained teachers are just a few notable examples. For these children, learning disabilities can add up and affect their success in the future.

In preschool, children may begin talking later than their peers, and when they do, they may have a small vocabulary and issues with pronunciation. Daily routine and instructions may be hard for them to follow. From kindergarten to fourth grade, children may appear to be poor spellers and often make errors while reading. Very importantly, they may also find it difficult to learn letter and sound connections, which is the cornerstone of reading and writing. Children who do not become proficient readers by third grade are four times more likely than their peers to fail to graduate from high school.

Students from fifth to eighth grade may demonstrate problems holding pens or pencils, making writing difficult. This stems from poor fine motor skills that tend to appear in the earlier grades. Additionally, they do not like to read aloud, nor do they like writing assignments. Issues with understanding facial expressions and body language may make it hard to make and maintain friendships.

A learning disability that goes unaddressed for years will generally start to show up as larger issues—especially because skills learned in school are meant to build upon each other, so failing to learn one means it will be increasingly difficult to learn the rest later. For these students, school can become an uncomfortable place.

If these issues are left unaddressed, they can make ninth to twelfth grade the most challenging years. Earlier issues that stem from learning disabilities continue to compound in these later years. Spelling and reading levels can be well below their peers, and the avoidance of writing and reading assignments generally means they get poor grades in their classes. Test-taking, which requires skills in math, reading, writing, summarizing, and remembering facts, can be incredibly difficult and stressful.

not make progress, the teacher tries more intensive small-group instruction.

In cases where a child is still struggling to master new concepts and lessons, such as letter-sound associations, a support teacher will work with the student either individually or in an even smaller group. If a student continues to struggle in this final stage of RTI, the school can then refer them for testing and evaluation to determine whether a learning disability exists. While RTI is primarily used in elementary schools, some high schools have adopted the approach as well. Furthermore, because the RTI approach focuses on smaller groups of children at a time, learning disabilities are more accurately identified. This allows schools to focus their special education resources on the students who need those services most.

Beginning an Evaluation

When students fail to respond to early interventions or when they are struggling and falling behind in class, teachers refer them for observation and testing to find out whether they are eligible for special education services. A team of school professionals, including a psychologist and a special educator, carry out the formal evaluation. Depending on the child's needs, the meeting may also include a speech and language therapist, an occupational therapist, or an adaptive physical education teacher for concerns about the child's fine and gross motor skills. The goal of an evaluation is to determine if the child qualifies for special education services, and if so, develop an individualized education program (IEP) for them. This is a specific, specially detailed plan that outlines annual academic and social goals for the individual student. IEPs are designed for each child's specific needs.

The process begins with a referral for an evaluation; frequently, the child's teacher makes the request either verbally or in writing. The child's parent or primary caregiver, however, makes the final decision for an evaluation. If a parent does not give their consent for an evaluation, then the process ends there. When consent is given, an evaluation is scheduled to take place either at the child's school or at a separate testing location. As the Eunice Kennedy Shriver National Institute of Child Health and Development explained, "Usually, several specialists work as a team to do the evaluation. The team may include a psychologist, a special education expert, and a speech-language pathologist. Many schools also have reading specialists who can help diagnose a reading disability."[33]

The evaluation has two main goals: determining whether or not a child has one or more disabilities as defined by IDEA and determining if special education services in school will benefit the child. A wide range of tests and methods can be used in the evaluation process. Many are standardized tests that the school has deemed accurate and reliable. These standardized tests are useful because they give evaluators a clear picture of how the child performs compared to other children their age. Observations of the child may occur in school or at home, allowing evaluators to see how the child typically behaves in these settings. Interviews also take place during this process, with parents and teachers providing information that will help in the evaluators' final decision.

The child's medical history is sometimes used during the evaluation process as well, which helps determine whether or not a child is having difficulty learning due to a previous or current medical condition, such as poor eyesight or hearing. Evaluators also sometimes question the child in an attempt to find out what the child likes and how they feel about school in case the issue is simply a behavioral one. Finally, evaluators will also look at the child's progress during RTI. Records that were taken by the child's teacher during the RTI approach will show evaluators how certain teaching and reward methods were used in the classroom so they can pinpoint when and where those approaches stopped working for the child.

Developing a Child's IEP

At the end of the evaluation, the parents and evaluators meet to discuss the child's evaluation results. During this meeting, the parents will be notified on whether or not their child has a disability as outlined by IDEA. If they do, then the child is eligible for special education services. Once this occurs, a special team from the child's school will have 30 days to create an IEP for the child that addresses their unique needs.

In order for an IEP to be developed, the child's school must schedule a meeting to discuss a child's individual program. Parents, any school staff who are involved, and the IEP team itself attend this meeting. Together, they discuss the child's needs and specific goals that they would like the child to reach during the academic school year. The IEP must also include the support systems that will be set in place to help the child reach these goals, such as individual or

Once an IEP is written and goals are set, children will begin receiving services with a qualified therapist. These therapists can work with the child both at home and in school. For younger children, working with a therapist at home is sometimes better because the child is generally more comfortable in a familiar setting.

group-based services. These services can be scheduled daily, weekly, or monthly. When the IEP is completed, the child's teachers, parents, and service providers all receive a copy for their reference.

IEPs are a team effort; every adult involved has a specific and important role in ensuring that the IEP is being carried out effectively. Throughout the school year, teachers and service providers will inform parents about the child's performance, which is measured by when and how the child reaches the goals listed on their IEP. The IEP team will monitor and review every child's IEP at least once a year. After three years, the child must be re-evaluated. During this re-evaluation, it may be determined that the child requires continued individualized education services. In some cases, a child may reach the goals as outlined on their IEP and will no longer require further special education.

Section 504

Aside from IDEA, another law, called Section 504 of the Rehabilitation Act, also gives protection to students with disabilities. However, the support it provides is more general than an IEP. A 504 plan outlines what accommodations the student will receive from the school, but it does not have things it must include. This is unlike an IEP, which has specific areas that must, by law, be included. Additionally, the definition of disability is broader under Section 504 than IDEA, so a child who does not qualify for an IEP may still qualify for a 504 plan. Qualification is determined through evaluation by school officials. The disability must be severe enough to prevent the child from learning effectively in a normal classroom environment to qualify for either an IEP or a 504 plan.

Different Approaches to Reading

Most students with an IEP have a language-based learning disability, and one of the special education services they often need is extra reading support. In recent years, researchers have made dramatic progress in understanding what happens in the brain as people learn to read. They have discovered that the key to the entire reading process is a concept called "phonemic awareness," which is the understanding of how to manipulate the smallest units of sound, or phonemes, that are the building blocks of all spoken and written words. The word *cat*, for example, can be broken into the phonemes /k/, which sounds like *kuh*, /æ/, which sounds like *aaa*, and /t/, which sounds like *tuh*. Students with language-based learning disabilities may find it difficult to learn how to read, especially because their skills in comprehension, decoding, and phonemic awareness are not typically strong.

Researchers say that as early as preschool, there are ways to assess whether students struggle with phonemic awareness and to begin to address the problem right away with intensive small-group instruction. Many research-based reading programs are designed to help young children with reading disabilities. Two of the best known are called the Orton-Gillingham approach and the Lindamood-Bell learning process. In the Orton-Gillingham approach, lessons are highly structured and designed to follow a specific order. In schools that use this program, students work in small groups made up of other students who all have similar skills. Orton-Gillingham uses a multisensory approach to reading by engaging a child's senses, teaching letters through sound, sight, movement, and touch.

Lindamood-Bell shares similar ideas with Orton-Gillingham but is not as widely used by schools. While this approach also teaches by engaging a student's senses, Lindamood-Bell takes this one step further by encouraging students to create mental images of the words they learn. Upon learning how to read the word "elephant," for example, their teacher may ask the child to describe and imagine the elephant in different ways. By doing this, children are more likely to make lasting mental connections to the words they learn. Besides mental imagery, this approach also teaches children to learn how phonemes feel as they are physically formed with the lips, tongue, and palate (the roof of the mouth).

These approaches are just two of many different teaching techniques and methods that are currently in use around the United States. Some of them stem from the Orton-Gillingham approach, such as the Wilson Reading System and the Barton Reading Program. In comparison, the Lindamood-Bell process is not as widely used. While the program does partner with some public schools, it is largely only available in private schools that not all families can afford. However, there is no single perfect approach to teaching reading, as everyone learns in different ways. As the LDA explained, "No single reading method will be effective for all students with learning disabilities. Most individuals with learning disabilities will benefit from the application of a variety of methods."[34]

When Do IEPs End?

For some students, learning disabilities are not discovered until they are in high school. Even then, it is not too late for them to request and receive special education services such as IEPs. IDEA requires the IEP team to allow high school students to attend and take part in their own IEP meetings if they want to, and teens are encouraged to do this so they learn self-advocacy skills, which are the ability to make their needs and wants known. The idea is to provide students with skills that will continue to benefit them in their adult lives.

Between the ages of 14 and 16, the student will work with their school's IEP team to create a transition plan, which provides the student with a framework of how to continue achieving their goals after high school. The transition plan also lists skills that the student will need to function in everyday life, such as time and money management. IDEA only covers students until they graduate high school or reach the age of 22, whichever comes first. The student's parents no longer have any legal say in their child's IEP decisions once the student turns 18. At that age, the student is legally an adult and must make all decisions and requests by themselves.

Every high school student with an IEP will leave school with what is called a Summary of Performance, or SOP. The SOP is a document that summarizes the student's academic achievements as well as the skills they have learned—or still need to learn—in order to succeed after high school. Because colleges have different legal obligations than high schools, no IEPs or special education services exist after high school. Colleges must, however, still follow the ADA and other laws that affect people with disabilities. Many colleges offer accommodations such as designated note-takers, and professors are required to work with students who have a learning disability to figure out how best to accommodate their specific needs. However, this cannot happen if the student does not

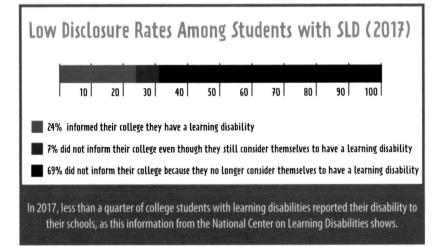

Low Disclosure Rates Among Students with SLD (2017)

| 10 | 20 | 30 | 40 | 50 | 60 | 70 | 80 | 90 | 100 |

24% informed their college they have a learning disability

7% did not inform their college even though they still consider themselves to have a learning disability

69% did not inform their college because they no longer consider themselves to have a learning disability

In 2017, less than a quarter of college students with learning disabilities reported their disability to their schools, as this information from the National Center on Learning Disabilities shows.

inform their university of their disability, which is why learning self-advocacy skills in high school is so important.

A Changing Landscape

Research on math disabilities has not received nearly the level of attention as research on reading disabilities, and special education services themselves might be to blame. According to Dr. Kate Garnett, "While children with disorders in mathematics are specifically included under the definition of Learning Disabilities, seldom do math learning difficulties cause children to be referred for evaluation. In many school systems, special education services are provided almost exclusively on the basis of children's reading disabilities."[35] It is for this reason that some parents and teachers may think that math disabilities are not as common as reading disabilities. Learning disabilities in math do exist, though, and they can have serious, long-lasting effects on people.

Researchers from Western Michigan University confirmed this in January 2018. They explained, "Analyses in both the United Kingdom (UK) and United States (US) revealed that poor numeracy skills impacted employment opportunities and wages, even in the presence of adequate literacy skills."[36] In other words, although many adults with learning disabilities had strong reading and language skills, their poor math skills affected their ability to hold jobs and earn higher wages. New studies such as this one are aiming to change the way schools are handling learning disabilities by creating new recommendations for teaching and further studying the underlying causes of math learning disabilities.

Many accommodations and tools currently exist for students with learning disabilities, even math-related ones. One of the most important supports for students is having a well-trained tutor or teacher. This helps ensure that students are mastering the correct skills instead of repeating the same mistakes when completing math problems. Other methods include making math problems relatable to everyday experiences to make math concepts more concrete. Because success in math is strongly dependent on having good reading skills, children with learning disabilities in reading often suffer similar issues in math. As research continues to expand and shed new light on better teaching methods, new techniques will likely be developed and old ones will be improved upon.

The Importance of Inclusion

As outlined by IDEA, children with disabilities have a right to learn in the least restrictive environment possible. In many schools, this means they will spend their days in an inclusion classroom. In this type of classroom, even students with math and reading disabilities who need extra support spend most or even all of their day with their nondisabled classmates. The general education teacher collaborates closely with a special educator. Together, they work to ensure that every child's academic goals, regardless of abilities, are eventually met. Students take part in cooperative learning projects in which they work together and develop social relationships with everyone in the class, but they also often break into small groups for reading or math activities according to their ability levels.

Inclusion classrooms have many benefits. One of them is that the stigma of having a learning disability is lessened because these students are not singled out from the rest of their classmates. This leads to a better sense of self-esteem and reduced stress in the classroom. Furthermore, inclusion classrooms use a variety of different teaching strategies and resources. These strategies and resources benefit not only the children with learning disabilities, but the others as well. Finally, special education students in these classrooms do not typically need to be pulled out of the room for special services such as speech or occupational therapy. Because a special education teacher is always in the classroom, constant and consistent support is available to all of the students.

Inclusion classrooms for children are a right, not a privilege. Years ago, schools would separate children with a learning disability from their peers. People did not understand why children demonstrated

Everyone Learns Differently

Every child learns differently in the classroom, and every teacher teaches differently as well. There are many types of preferences that students, especially those with learning disabilities, have in regard to learning. Following these preferences generally makes learning much easier.

Auditory learners work best using speaking and musical memory techniques. These are the students who generally like to read out loud, participate in classroom discussions, and create short songs or mnemonic devices to memorize information for tests. A mnemonic device is a pattern of letters or ideas that help someone remember something; for example, many people remember the order of the planets in the solar system with the sentence "My Very Educated Mother Just Served Us Noodles" because the first letter of each word in the sentence is the same as the first letter of the planets' names.

Visual learners remember information best when there are visual cues to go along with it. These students highlight and illustrate their notes in class, and they enjoy studying by viewing clips, videos, and pictures that are related to the material being taught.

Tactile learners are the ones who learn through touch and movement. These students generally like to stand at their desk as they learn, and they enjoy having something to do with their hands, such as squeezing clay or playing with fidget spinners. They also benefit from taking frequent breaks.

Studies have found that the way the brain is structured is strongly linked to learning preference, with the left hemisphere of the brain assisting in auditory processing and the right hemisphere assisting in visual processing. Learning disabilities have been found to affect these specific parts of the brain. As understanding increases, so can the quality of teaching methods in the classroom.

lack of attention or disrupted the classroom, and at that time, they felt that the best solution was to separate the students they viewed as "problem children" from everybody else. Today, however, schools recognize that these behaviors stem from learning disabilities that are treatable. Inclusion classrooms ensure that all children, regardless of ability, have an equal chance of succeeding in school. This is due to years of advocating for new laws, policies, resources, and funding to make changes in education. Inclusion classrooms are successful because they encourage a welcoming environment for every student.

The Importance of Good Teaching

According to the LDA, "Success for the student with learning disabilities requires a focus on individual achievement, individual progress, and individual learning. This requires specific, directed, individualized, intensive remedial instruction for students who are struggling."[37] Having a learning disability can turn the classroom into a stressful and uncomfortable place to be. Research continues to show that learning takes place best in an environment that is welcoming, free from judgment, and inclusive. The teacher is the key to creating such an environment.

By recognizing individual differences and understanding the intellectual and emotional needs of every child, teachers help ensure their students' success. For a child with a learning disability, the need for this type of highly trained and responsive teacher cannot be understated. Although today there are a wide range of methods, techniques, and learning styles being used in schools across America, it is important to realize that the fight for high-quality, equal education is far from over. Some schools simply do not have the resources to provide high-quality

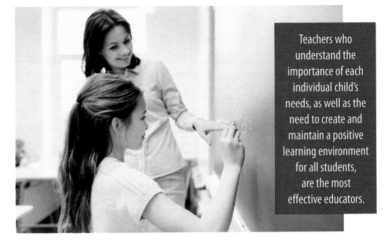

Teachers who understand the importance of each individual child's needs, as well as the need to create and maintain a positive learning environment for all students, are the most effective educators.

special education programs; economic and racial gaps still exist in schools across the country.

Countless teachers, parents, doctors, researchers, school administrators, and politicians continue to work tirelessly on behalf of children with learning disabilities. New and ongoing research studies lead to new theories and advancements in teaching methods, increasing the public's knowledge of learning disabilities. Special education is effective when it is a high-quality program, and students of these programs largely benefit from them. However, learning disabilities are still lifelong, which means that children with learning disabilities need to learn how to adapt to them in order to function well as adults in everyday life.

CHAPTER FIVE

LEARNING DISABILITIES AFTER HIGH SCHOOL

The reality for children with learning disabilities is that they will grow up to become adults with learning disabilities; learning disabilities cannot be outgrown. The difficulties these children experience will affect them when they graduate from high school and move on to college or into the workplace. As adults, learning disabilities can make life difficult. Memory, organization, and social skills are just as necessary in an adult's everyday life as in a child's. Furthermore, problems with math and language skills can affect their work lives. Dyslexia, for example, might make some adults avoid writing important emails at work. Dyscalculia could make managing finances difficult and lead to inaccurate measurements in cooking or construction work.

The effects of learning disabilities can have far-reaching implications as children enter adulthood. As the National Center for Learning Disabilities reported in 2014, many adults with learning disabilities "struggle with underachievement and underemployment, have few friends and, with greater frequency than their non-LD peers, appear to end up in trouble with the law."[38] The Center also reported that employment rates for adults with learning disabilities declined from 55 percent to 46 percent between 2005 and 2010, and that "forty-one percent of young adults with LD (within eight years of leaving high school) complete any type of postsecondary education compared to a completion rate of 52 percent for the general population."[39]

An adult with a learning disability might find completing work reports and sending important emails to be stressful. Fortunately, accommodations can be made for them in the workplace.

For people with learning disabilities, achieving success in their personal and professional lives may depend on whether they can learn to accept their disabilities and adapt to living with them. In recent years, many opportunities have opened up for adults with learning disabilities in areas of life that once would have been closed to them. These opportunities are made possible through assistive technology and other accommodations that can be made in everyday life, including at colleges and workplaces. Increasingly, students with learning disabilities continue to graduate from high school and enroll in public and private colleges and universities. As adults, they are entering fields such as business, entertainment, medicine, education, the arts, media, science, and technology.

Adults with learning disabilities can achieve success in their personal and professional lives by asking for the support and accommodations they need. Seeking the help and encouragement of others, such as supportive family members, friends, teachers, and colleagues, is beneficial as well. Having strong coping strategies to deal with frustration and failure is also important, as is knowing what kinds of services are available to them. The ADA was designed to prevent workplace discrimination and allow access to workplace accommodations, but only an estimated 5 percent of young adults with learning disabilities reported receiving these accommodations in a 2014 survey. Increasing public knowledge is important because every person with a learning disability deserves to benefit from the services that are available to them.

Life Without an IEP

In some special education programs, students have begun to accept and understand the nature of their learning disabilities long before they graduate from high school. Once a student turns 16, their school IEP must include a statement of how they will transition into adulthood. This statement reflects their own goals and visions for their lives as adults. Around this time, they are also encouraged to consider whether college is the right path for them. In 2014, the LDA reported that an estimated 75 percent of students with learning disabilities had a transition plan in their IEP. Furthermore, more than 50 percent of these students planned to attend college after high school, and 67 percent of them did so—the same percentage as their nondisabled peers. However, twice as many students with learning disabilities chose to attend two-year colleges compared with their nondisabled peers, who were more likely to attend a four-year school.

Some students with learning disabilities find college life relatively easy. They may have to study harder than others, but they also have a few advantages over their peers who do not have learning disabilities. Most have been evaluated in high school and have gained insights about how they learn best, which may not have been the case for someone without a learning disability. They are also likely to have encountered situations in which they were forced to advocate for themselves, so they are sometimes less hesitant than other students to approach professors when they need help.

For other students with learning disabilities, the transition can be rocky. Some may feel suddenly overwhelmed with the academic demands of college life, especially in the absence of the goals and supports of an IEP, which some have had since early childhood. Additionally, underdeveloped social skills may make it difficult for them to make new friends and live with roommates. Those who have always relied on their parents to advocate for them may be unprepared to fight their own academic battles.

Under the terms of the ADA, it is illegal for colleges and professors to specifically ask students about their disabilities. It is also illegal for colleges to deny acceptance to any student because of a disability. Students with learning disabilities, just like every other applicant, must meet the school's individual criteria for admissions. Furthermore, if they want access to accommodations for the classroom and exams, they must voluntarily disclose their disabilities. These accommodations, however, are not automatically granted. Students need to meet the school's requirements for such requests, which generally include some type of official proof of their disability. This is done to ensure that no one without a disability is taking advantage of the accommodation system to get benefits they do not need.

Learning Disabilities in the Workforce

Even in a job that is well suited to their needs, people with learning disabilities often face challenges in the workplace. They may take longer than their colleagues to accomplish a task or grow overwhelmed trying to keep up with deadlines and heavy work-

Reasonable Accommodations in College

When students do disclose their disabilities, college officials are legally bound to provide reasonable accommodations. The term "reasonable" is not clearly defined in the ADA, which is why a student's self-awareness and self-advocacy skills are incredibly important. Students are far more likely to succeed in college if they can explain their needs clearly and ask professors for accommodations. Some of these accommodations in college may include:

• providing a note-taker for the student

• providing services such as proofreading and editing

• extending the allotted amount of time to complete assignments and exams

• breaking large assignments and exams down into more manageable sections

• captioning any videos shown as part of a class

• modifying testing formats

• allowing the student to record lectures instead of taking notes

Colleges will not change the content of an exam for students with learning disabilities, nor are they legally required to. They are, however, legally responsible for covering the costs of any accommodations that are made, including any equipment that is required. No student will have to pay for any of these, and they will not be charged more for a program if they have a learning disability. These reasonable accommodations are intended to make the learning process equal for all students, regardless of their abilities.

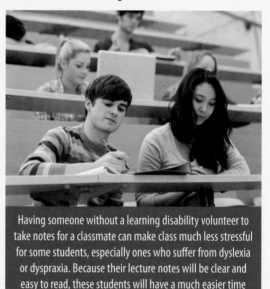

Having someone without a learning disability volunteer to take notes for a classmate can make class much less stressful for some students, especially ones who suffer from dyslexia or dyspraxia. Because their lecture notes will be clear and easy to read, these students will have a much easier time studying them.

loads. If they have a language-learning disability, they may have trouble writing reports, taking messages, or reading instructions. They may also feel frustrated or worry about the stigma of having a learning disability, although there are several laws that protect learning-disabled adults in the workplace. Just like in a college setting, an adult does not legally have to disclose their learning disability. They may choose to withhold this information for a variety of reasons, but by doing so, they may miss out on accommodations that can be of great help to them.

The ADA forbids employers from discriminating against qualified individuals with disabilities in hiring, firing, promotion, salary, or other conditions of employment. The only exception to this rule is if the disability would prevent someone from doing a job even with accommodations. For some, the ways they have adapted to living with their learning disabilities make their disability unnoticeable to others. Others choose to disclose their learning disability if it begins to affect their job performance. In those cases, the employer can offer to make reasonable accommodations to assist the worker in performing their job duties. This is best done sooner rather than later, because as the Equal Employment Opportunity Commission explains, "an employer is not required to

Employers cannot legally discriminate against individuals with learning disabilities by refusing to hire them. However, it is important that these individuals request reasonable accommodations if they believe their disabilities could negatively impact their job performance.

Reasonable Accommodations in the Workplace

While employees with learning disabilities must meet the educational and skill requirements of a job, they are entitled to accommodations that will make their work successful. Any accommodation requests that would create a financial hardship for an employer do not have to be accepted. Luckily, accommodations that employers can make in the workplace are often easy and affordable changes to make, which is why they are called reasonable accommodations.

Employers may agree to:

• provide extra training or a mentor to guide the employee upon being hired

• encourage the use of electronic reminders through computer calendars or smartphone apps for deadlines and other important information

• encourage employees to design and arrange their workspaces to meet their individual needs—for example, by using colored organizers, flowcharts, and checklists

• provide speech-to-text and text-to-speech software on workplace computers

• modify the employee's work schedule within reason, such as providing short, periodic breaks

Employers must follow a wide range of guidelines to comply with the ADA. These guidelines help create a fair workplace and ensure that their employees find success in their jobs.

A workplace accommodation can be as easy as letting an employee design their workspace to meet their needs or giving them things such as checklists, chart organizers, and sticky notes. These changes are not expensive, and they can make a world of difference to workers with learning disabilities.

excuse performance problems that occurred prior to the accommodation request."[40]

Workers with a learning disability are not a risk to have in the workplace, despite any negative social stigmas that may exist. Research has shown that workers with learning disabilities often have a great work ethic and tend to stay with the same organization for longer periods of time. The employer receives some benefits from hiring these employees as well, such as increased productivity and tax benefits for the company.

The Increasing Importance of Assistive Technology

Adults with learning disabilities often meet the challenges of a job or college course with the help of assistive technologies (ATs). An AT is any device used by a person with learning or physical disabilities that improves their ability to perform everyday functions. The use of these technologies is supported in IDEA, thanks to revisions made to the law in 1997 and 2004. Such technologies can range from low-tech equipment such as graphic organizers to more high-tech personal computing systems, such as voice recognition software. ATs open up job and educational opportunities for people with learning disabilities where few previously existed, and since some are very inexpensive to put in place, poverty is often not a barrier to using them. A wide range of ATs are used in schools and workplaces around the country.

On the low-tech end, a simple timer can provide a student with a visual indicator of how much time is left on an activity, making their transition to the next task easier. Similarly, pencil grips can help make writing more comfortable, and the use of inflatable seat cushions in the classroom can help calm children who suffer from attention and sensory processing issues. High-tech tools can be especially beneficial for those with math and writing disabilities. For example, portable word processors allow students with dyslexia to type their work in class instead of handwriting it, while variable-speed voice recorders allow students to record lectures. During study sessions, students can play back these recordings and change the speed and pitch of the teacher's voice to better understand it if needed. Unfortunately, some ATs are expensive, making them unavailable to people who do not have a lot of money. However, in some cases, schools may be able to provide these devices until a student graduates.

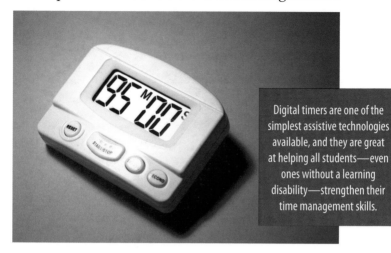

Digital timers are one of the simplest assistive technologies available, and they are great at helping all students—even ones without a learning disability—strengthen their time management skills.

Calculators, in particular, can also range from low-tech to high-tech, with some models providing text-to-speech features for students with dyscalculia. This allows numbers in problems and equations to be read correctly out loud, reducing the risk of a student making a mistake. Of course, no single AT is perfect for every learning disability. Students with learning disabilities need to find the AT or combination of ATs that best suit their needs and enhance their learning.

Life with a Learning Disability

Even with ATs for support, learning disabilities can interfere with everyday tasks that most people do not think twice about, such as grocery shopping or leaving a tip on a restaurant bill. These disabilities can also make it difficult to carry out more important tasks, such as making financial decisions, keeping track of medications, driving, or forming strong friendships. The solutions to these problems may be as simple as always taking a list to the grocery store or posting a chart with medical information in the kitchen, or as complicated as learning how to interpret nonverbal facial expressions. Adults with learning disabilities sometimes need to seek the support of social workers, job counselors, or psychologists to help them develop social skills or overcome their frustration and anxiety in the workplace.

For adults whose disabilities are severe, living independently can be a real challenge. If they have motor disabilities, they may not be able to drive and may have to rely on public transportation, such as buses and subways. If their disabilities involve math, they may struggle to use money and credit cards properly. If they lack basic reading skills, they may be unable to read instructions, follow signs, or hold a steady job. Some studies have even found a

Adult Learning Disability Assessments

There are many adults who never received a learning disability diagnosis as a child, which means they never received the support they needed in school to reach their maximum potential. While they may have adapted and managed to get by for a long time, some of these adults may have difficulty reaching their goals in college, their careers, and everyday life. If they or a family member suspects that a learning disability might be to blame, they can be tested for one, even as an adult. These assessments can be done in a variety of local settings, from colleges and universities—including hospitals or clinics that partner with such universities—to regional organizations that are affiliated with the LDA.

Adult learning disability assessments are not too different from the type of assessments children receive. They begin with a screening of the person's work, school, and medical history before moving on to an evaluation that tests their processing and intelligence skills. After the screening and evaluation is completed, a diagnosis can be made that identifies which, if any, learning disability the adult has. From there, resources and information can be provided to the person to help them achieve the support they need in school, work, and day-to-day life. While the price of these assessments can vary by location and other factors, some insurance companies will cover the costs. Some clinics and schools may also charge only a small fee or no fee at all, as these assessments are part of their academic research programs.

correlation between learning disabilities and the like-lihood of developing a psychiatric disorder such as anxiety. This means that in addition to ATs and other support services, some people also need to make use of services that are available to manage and treat these disorders, such as the help of a therapist, psychiatrist, or prescribed medication.

A Network of Support

Adults who refuse to let their disabilities dominate their lives often have a support network of family and friends who accept and encourage them along the way. These people are there to listen and offer support without reacting harshly or making judg-ments. At the same time, they guide their loved one with a learning disability toward realistic goals and expectations. Frequently, parents continue to advo-cate for their children as they grow. They are the ones who navigate the pain of struggling in school and give children the academic and emotional support to thrive. In some cases, they may have experienced disappointment, denial, or—if they have a disabili-ty themselves—guilt when they first learned of their child's difficulties, but a truly supportive parent will overcome those feelings to give their child the help they need to succeed.

There is a dialogue that should exist between fami-ly members as well, as everyone can have a role in sup-porting a loved one with a learning disability, whether they are a child or an adult. Some might begin by discussing the history of learning disabilities in the family, providing insight and answers to old questions. For example, an adult who has always struggled with reading but never received a formal dyslexia diagno-sis might discover that their grandfather had similar difficulties. This discovery might prompt the person to take a learning disability assessment. Coping skills are also very important within families. Families who work together can provide individuals who have a learning disability with emotional support as well as guidance with everyday life skills well into adulthood.

By discussing a child's needs and goals, parents of children with learning disabilities can better understand the disability and provide more appropriate emotional, social, and academic support.

These kinds of families learn to be flexible in their expectations and help ensure that their children with learning disabilities reach their maximum potential as adults. For some people with learning disabilities, their siblings, teachers, coaches, friends, and coworkers play a similar role in encouraging and supporting them. Adults with learning disabilities, especially those who do not have parents, family members, or friends to advise and encourage them may turn to groups that offer support and advocate on their behalf. Many of these groups, including the LDA and the National Center for Learning Disabilities, connect them with others who face similar challenges so they can discuss their life experiences. They also provide legal advice in cases of workplace discrimination or direct people to vocational training and career support services. Support groups can also frequently be found online; many have online forums where people can post questions and advice from all around the world.

Advocating for a Better Tomorrow

Every year, new theories, technologies, services, and policies are created to ensure better lives for all individuals with learning disabilities. People from all backgrounds—many of them with learning disabilities themselves—tirelessly advocate for better funding, better rights, and better education for those who live with a learning disability. While schools and the workplace are in a much better place than they were 50 years ago, there is still much more work to be done to ensure stronger equality in education, work, and everyday life. The key to a better tomorrow for the learning-disabled population relies on changing public perception: There are quite simply too many misconceptions, labels, and stigmas associated with having a learning disability.

Studies continue to demonstrate that the general public has major misconceptions about learning disabilities, such as the reasons why these disabilities occur and the belief that they correspond with a person's IQ score. Nearly 67 percent of respondents in a 2012 survey knew nothing about dyscalculia and dysgraphia, while more than 90 percent of them were familiar with dyslexia. Some wrongly attributed the development of learning disabilities to poor diets and too much screen time. There are also many people who keep their learning disabilities a secret, which contributes to the idea that they are rare or that intelligent people do not have them. Part of the reason for this secrecy is that sometimes those who speak up are still made fun of for behaviors that are not their fault. Improving public knowledge and perception is an extremely important part of improving the lives of people with learning disabilities around the world, allowing them to feel more comfortable requesting services and accommodations that can— and should—be made for them. Despite the changes that have occurred over the past few decades, there is still much work to be done. Recently, the National Center for Learning Disabilities recommended beginning screening for learning disabilities earlier in a child's life, reducing the amount of discipline used with children who have learning disabilities—for example, redirecting them instead of punishing them when their attention wanders—and investing more in public schools, among other things.

Learning disabilities are not a curse. In fact, in some ways, learning disabilities can actually be a blessing. As Daniel Radcliffe said, "It has never held me back, and some of the smartest people I know are people who have learning disabilities. The fact that some things are more of a struggle will only make you more determined, harder working and more imaginative in the solutions you find to problems."[41]

NOTES

Introduction: Hidden Disabilities

1. "About Learning Disabilities," Eunice Kennedy Shriver National Institute of Human Health and Development, last updated September 11, 2018. www.nichd.nih.gov/health/topics/learning/conditioninfo/default.

2. "About Learning Disabilities," Eunice Kennedy Shriver National Institute of Human Health and Development.

3. "Types of Learning Disabilities," Learning Disabilities Association of America, accessed on October 15, 2018. ldaamerica.org/types-of-learning-disabilities/.

4. "About Learning Disabilities," Eunice Kennedy Shriver National Institute of Human Health and Development.

5. Candace Cortiella and Sheldon H. Horowitz, *The State of Learning Disabilities: Facts, Trends and Emerging Issues*. New York, NY: National Center for Learning Disabilities, 2014. www.ncld.org/wp-content/uploads/2014/11/2014-State-of-LD.pdf.

Chapter One: A Complicated Definition

6. Quoted in "Five Misconceptions About Learning Disabilities," PBS *NewsHour*, March 16, 2012. www.pbs.org/newshour/health/five-misconceptions-about-learning-disabilities.

7. Larry Silver, "What Are Learning Disabilities?," LD Online, 2001. www.ldonline.org/article/5821.

8. "Brain Basics: The Life and Death of a Neuron," National Institute of Neurological Disorders and Stroke, last updated November 6, 2018. www.ninds.nih.gov/Disorders/Patient-Caregiver-Education/Life-and-Death-Neuron.

9. Deborah Bach, "Research Shows Brain Differences in Children with Dyslexia and Dysgraphia," University of Washington, April 28, 2015. www.washington.edu/news/2015/04/28/research-shows-brain-differences-in-children-with-dyslexia-and-dysgraphia/.

10. "Theoretical Perspectives on the Causes of Learning Disabilities," National Association of Special Education Teachers, accessed on October 15, 2018. www.naset.org/fileadmin/user_upload/LD_Report/Issue__2_LD_Report_Theoretical_Perspectives_Causes.pdf.

11. "Causes of Learning Disabilities," PBS, accessed on October 15, 2018. www.pbs.org/parents/education/learning-disabilities/basics/causes/.

12. Bob Cunningham, "Do Boys Have Learning and Attention Issues More Often Than Girls?," Understood, accessed on October 15, 2018. www.understood.org/en/learning-attention-issues/getting-started/what-you-need-to-know/do-boys-have-learning-and-attention-issues-more-often-than-girls.

13. Cunningham, "Do Boys Have Learning and Attention Issues More Often Than Girls?"

14. Cortiella and Horowitz, *The State of Learning Disabilities.*

Chapter Two:
Exploring Learning Disabilities

15. Quoted in "Dyslexia Defined: New Yale Study 'Uncouples' Reading and IQ Over Time," Yale School of Medicine, December 17, 2009. medicine.yale.edu/news/article.aspx?id=1479.

16. Erica Patino, "Understanding Dysgraphia," Understood, accessed on October 22, 2018. www.understood.org/en/learning-attention-issues/child-learning-disabilities/dysgraphia/understanding-dysgraphia.

17. Erica Patino, "Understanding Dyspraxia," Understood, accessed on October 22, 2018. www.understood.org/en/learning-attention-issues/child-learning-disabilities/dyspraxia/understanding-dyspraxia.

18. "Executive Functioning," Learning Disabilities Association of America, accessed on October 22, 2018. ldaamerica.org/types-of-learning-disabilities/executive-functioning/.

19. "ADHD," Learning Disabilities Association of America, accessed on October 22, 2018. ldaamerica.org/types-of-learning-disabilities/adhd/.

20. "Attention-Deficit/Hyperactivity Disorder (ADHD)," Centers for Disease Control and Prevention, September 28, 2018. www.cdc.gov/ncbddd/adhd/research.html#ref1.

Chapter Three:
From "Word-Blind" to "Dyslexic"

21. "A Brief History of the Disability Rights Movement," Anti-Defamation League, accessed on October 22, 2018. www.adl.org/education/resources/backgrounders/disability-rights-movement.

22. "History," Learning Disabilities Association of America, 2018. ldaamerica.org/about-us/history/.

23. "History of IDA," International Dyslexia Association, accessed on October 22, 2018. dyslexiaida.org/history-of-the-ida/.

24. Quoted in Victoria Jones, "When the Classroom Feels Hostile," Harvard Graduate School of Education, August 31, 2015. www.gse.harvard.edu/news/uk/15/08/when-classroom-feels-hostile.

25. Michael L. VanBlaricum, "Samuel Kirk," Illinois Distributed Museum, accessed on October 22, 2018. distributedmuseum.illinois.edu/exhibit/samuel_kirk/.

26. Dara Shifrer, Chandra Muller, and Rebecca Callahan, "Disproportionality and Learning Disabilities: Parsing Apart Race, Socioeconomic Status, and Language," *Journal of Learning Disabilities*, vol. 44, no. 3, 2011. www.ncbi.nlm.nih.gov/pmc/articles/PMC4133990/#.

27. "A Brief History of the Disability Rights Movement," Anti-Defamation League.

28. Quoted in "Twenty-Five Years of Progress in Educating Children with Disabilities Through IDEA," U.S. Department of Education, July 19, 2007. www2.ed.gov/policy/speced/leg/idea/history.html.

Chapter Four:
The Key Question

29. Gerald R. Ford, "Statement on Signing the Education for All Handicapped Children Act of 1975," The American Presidency Project, December 2, 1975. www.presidency.ucsb.edu/ws/index.php?pid=5413.

30. Ford, "Statement on Signing the Education for All Handicapped Children Act of 1975."

31. "Definitions of Learning Disabilities," Learning Disabilities Association of Illinois, 2012. ldail.com/index.php?option=com_content&view=article&id=37:definitions&catid=11&Itemid=118.

32. Sally L. Smith, "Parenting Children with Learning Disabilities, ADHD, and Related Disorders," Learning Disabilities Association of America, 2002. ldaamerica.org/what-do-parents-of-children-with-learning-disabilities-adhd-and-related-disorders-deal-with/.

33. "How Are Learning Disabilities Diagnosed?," Eunice Kennedy Shriver National Institute of Human Health and Development, last updated September 11, 2018. www.nichd.nih.gov/health/topics/learning/conditioninfo/diagnosed.

34. Learning Disabilities Association of America, "Reading Methods for Students with LD," Reading Rockets, accessed on October 23, 2018. www.readingrockets.org/article/reading-methods-students-ld.

35. Kate Garnett, "Math Learning Disabilities," LD Online, 1998. www.ldonline.org/article/5896/.

36. Neelkamal Soares, Teresa Evans, and Dilip R. Patel, "Specific Learning Disability in Mathematics: A Comprehensive Review," *Transitional Pediatrics*, vol. 7, no. 1, 2018. www.ncbi.nlm. nih.gov/pmc/articles/PMC5803013/.

37. "Successful Strategies for Teaching Students with Learning Disabilities," Learning Disabilities Association of America, accessed on October 23, 2018. ldaamerica.org/successful-strategies-for-teaching-students-with-learning-disabilities/.

Chapter Five:
Learning Disabilities After High School

38. Cortiella and Horowitz, *The State of Learning Disabilities*.

39. Cortiella and Horowitz, *The State of Learning Disabilities*.

40. "The Americans with Disabilities Act: Applying Performance and Conduct Standards To Employees With Disabilities," U.S. Equal Employment Opportunity Commission, last updated December 20, 2017. www.eeoc.gov/ facts/performance-conduct.html.

41. Quoted in Geri Coleman Tucker, "'Harry Potter' Star Gives Dyspraxia Advice," Understood, December 16, 2014. www.understood.org/en/community-events/ blogs/in-the-news/2014/12/16/harry-potter-star-gives-dyspraxia-advice.

assistive technology (AT): Any technology used by people with learning or physical disabilities to perform tasks that might otherwise be difficult or impossible for them to complete.

central cortex: The part of the brain that directs the thinking and emotional functions. It is divided into halves called hemispheres that oversee all forms of conscious experience, including perception, language, motor skills, thinking skills, and organization skills. It is also called the cerebral cortex.

cognition: Thinking, or the mental processes by which knowledge and understanding are gained through reasoning, experience, and sense perception.

executive function: The set of mental processes that people use to regulate behaviors and accomplish tasks. Executive function is involved in planning, monitoring, organizing, evaluating, and adjusting course as needed to get a job done.

inclusion: An approach to educating students with learning and other disabilities in which students spend most or all of their time in a regular classroom with their nondisabled peers. A special educator collaborates with the classroom teacher on the disabled students' instruction. Inclusion is based on the rights of all children to participate fully in the classroom and to have access to the full curriculum.

individualized education program (IEP): A legally binding document that schools must create for students who qualify for special education. It is designed to meet the child's unique learning and social needs and describes goals, supports, and accommodations the child will receive to help them access the curriculum.

mainstreaming: The practice of educating students with disabilities in regular classrooms. In contrast to the inclusion model, there is little effort made to modify the curriculum or provide classroom supports to help students with learning disabilities gain better access to learning.

multisensory instruction: Instruction that engages all of the pathways of perception—including visual, auditory, and kinesthetic (movement)—to reinforce learning and short-term memory.

neurology: The branch of medical science that involves study of the nervous system and treatment of nervous system disorders.

neuron: A nerve cell.

phonemic awareness: The understanding of how to use and manipulate the smallest units of sound, or phonemes, which are the building blocks of all spoken and written words.

psychologist: A professional who studies human behavior and provides therapy and support for people with mental health and emotional issues. A school psychologist is involved in testing and evaluating students for learning disabilities. Psychologists are not authorized to prescribe medication.

special education: Instruction designed to meet the unique needs of students with learning and other disabilities. It involves individually planned and small-group instruction and monitoring of students' progress. Sometimes special education takes place in the regular classroom, but often it is handled in a school resource room.

special educator: A teacher, such as a reading or math specialist, who has been trained to work with students with learning and other disabilities.

ORGANIZATIONS TO CONTACT

Dyspraxia Foundation USA
1012 Windsor Road
Highland Park, IL 60035
(847) 780-3311
www.dyspraxiausa.org
This nonprofit organization based in Illinois aims to raise dyspraxia awareness by providing resources and personal stories for individuals who suffer from this neurological disorder. Its website includes fact sheets, information on dyspraxia symptoms, and links to international dyspraxia foundations from around the world.

International Dyslexia Association (IDA)
40 York Road, 4th Floor
Baltimore, MD 21204
(410) 296-0232
dyslexiaida.org
IDA is a nonprofit group that offers fact sheets, free webinars, and an online gallery featuring artwork from children with dyslexia and other learning disabilities. Its website even utilizes an in-browser assistive technology that uses text-to-speech software, allowing visitors with dyslexia to listen to the website's articles rather than read them.

Learning Disabilities Association of America (LDA)
4156 Library Road
Pittsburgh, PA 15234
(412) 341-1515
ldaamerica.org
LDA is a nonprofit volunteer organization that advocates for individuals with learning disabilities by funding research studies and working toward better rights and legislation. Its website provides free videos, webinars, informational tools, and ways to get involved with advocacy.

Project Eye-to-Eye
East Coast
50 Broad Street
Suite 1702
New York, NY 10004
(212) 537-4429
West Coast
2001 Center Street
Floor 4
Berkeley, CA 94704
(628) 400-4106
eyetoeyenational.org
This national award-winning mentor program began
in 1998 when college students with learning disabilities
from Brown University met with similar elementary
school students in Rhode Island. Today, this nonprofit
group offers mentor-training programs and chapters
across the United States. Information can be found on
the website about the group's free documentary film and
its educational phone app that aims to empower students
with learning disabilities.

**U.S. Department of Education Office of Special
Education and Rehabilitative Services (OSERS)**
400 Maryland Avenue SW
Washington, DC 20202-7100
(202) 245-7468
www2.ed.gov/about/offices/list/osers/osep/index.html
A division of the U.S. Department of Education,
this government agency supports programs that provide
legal protection to millions of individuals with learning
disabilities across the country. It guides research
studies and publishes statistics as well as informational
materials. Its Transition Steering Committee helps to
prepare students with learning disabilities for their move
from high school into college and the workforce.

Books

Biggs, Victoria. *Caged in Chaos: A Dyspraxic Guide to Breaking Free (Updated Edition)*. London, UK: Jessica Kingsley Publishers, 2014.
This inspiring and humorous nonfiction book serves as a guide for teens who are living with dyspraxia.

Hirschman, Catherine, and R. Christine Melton. *Backwords Forword: My Journey Through Dyslexia*. Hirschman Publishing, 2011.
Personal stories and factual information about dyslexia provide an interesting insight into this family's life.

Moss, Wendy L., and Denise M. Campbell. *The Survival Guide for Kids in Special Education (And Their Parents): Understanding What Special Ed Is & How It Can Help You*. Minneapolis, MN: Free Spirit Publishing, 2017.
In this handy and engaging guide, tips for self-advocacy, improving self-esteem, and completing self-assessment activities are provided as tools for students with learning disabilities and their parents.

Simpson, Cynthia, and Vicky Spencer. *College Success for Students with Learning Disabilities*. Waco, TX: Prufrock Press, 2009.
This book gives college-bound students resources, strategies, and support that will help them develop self-advocacy skills and provide them with guidance as they plan their transition from high school to college.

Websites

Friends of Quinn
friendsofquinn.com
An online community resource for young adults created by
Quinn Bradlee, a filmmaker and author who suffers from
learning disabilities, this website features tips for self-esteem,
self-advocacy, and stress management for teens with learning
disabilities as well as guidance for their parents and caregivers.

LDonline
www.ldonline.org
This website about learning disabilities includes videos, professional
advice and resources, first-person essays, children's artwork, and links
to related websites and organizations.

National Center for Learning Disabilities
www.ncld.org
This website offers information and resources for individuals with
learning disabilities, their parents, teachers, and other professionals.

TeensHealth: Learning Disabilities
kidshealth.org/en/teens/learning-disabilities.html
This section of the TeensHealth website features basic learning
disability information as well as homework and testing tips.
The articles on each page can be listened to using the assistive
text-to-speech reader.

Understood
www.understood.org/en
Discussion groups, tutorials, and free live expert chats are
offered daily on this website. There is also a unique learning
disability "simulator," which allows people to perform different
school activities through the eyes and ears of a child with a
learning disability.

INDEX

ABOUT THE AUTHOR

Peter Kogler has been an elementary school teacher in Buffalo, New York for the past 10 years. Having experienced learning disabilities with his students firsthand, he could not pass up the opportunity to work on such an important and relevant topic. When Peter is not teaching, he can usually be found reading, writing, watching movies, and collecting all things movie-related. This is his third book for Lucent Press.